Those Wonderful ECK Masters

Also by Harold Klemp

Animals Are Soul Too!
The Art of Spiritual Dreaming
Ask the Master, Books 1 and 2
Autobiography of a Modern Prophet
Child in the Wilderness
A Cosmic Sea of Words: The ECKANKAR Lexicon
Is Life a Random Walk?
The Living Word, Books 1 and 2
A Modern Prophet Answers Your Key Questions about Life
Past Lives, Dreams, and Soul Travel
Soul Travelers of the Far Country
The Spiritual Exercises of ECK
The Spiritual Laws of Life
The Temple of ECK
The Wind of Change
Wisdom of the Heart, Books 1 and 2
Your Road Map to the ECK Teachings: ECKANKAR Study Guide
Youth Ask a Modern Prophet about Life, Love, and God

The Mahanta Transcripts Series

Journey of Soul, Book 1
How to Find God, Book 2
The Secret Teachings, Book 3
The Golden Heart, Book 4
Cloak of Consciousness, Book 5
Unlocking the Puzzle Box, Book 6
The Eternal Dreamer, Book 7
The Dream Master, Book 8
We Come as Eagles, Book 9
The Drumbeat of Time, Book 10
What Is Spiritual Freedom? Book 11
How the Inner Master Works, Book 12
The Slow Burning Love of God, Book 13
The Secret of Love, Book 14
Our Spiritual Wake-Up Calls, Book 15
How to Survive Spiritually in Our Times, Book 16

The Immortality of Soul Series

The Language of Soul
Love—The Keystone of Life

Stories to Help You See God in Your Life

The Book of ECK Parables, Volume 1
The Book of ECK Parables, Volume 2
The Book of ECK Parables, Volume 3
Stories to Help You See God in Your Life, ECK Parables, Book 4

This book has been authored by and published under the supervision of the Mahanta, the Living ECK Master, Sri Harold Klemp. It is the Word of ECK.

Those Wonderful ECK Masters

Harold Klemp

ECKANKAR
Minneapolis

Those Wonderful ECK Masters

Copyright © 2005 ECKANKAR

Printed in U.S.A.
Edited by Joan Klemp, Anthony Moore, Mary Carroll Moore
Cover illustration by Don McFadden
Cover design by Stan Burgess
Text illustrations by Helen Baird, Ann Hubert,
Dimce Stojanovski, Paul Twitchell
Spine photo by Robert Huntley

Library of Congress Cataloging-in-Publication

Klemp, Harold.
    Those wonderful ECK masters / Harold Klemp.
       p. cm.
    ISBN 1-57043-217-1 (pbk. : alk. paper)
    1. Eck masters. 2. Spiritual life—Eckankar (Organization) I. Title.

BP605.E3K5747 2005
299'.93—dc22
                                      2005009837

♾ This paper meets the requirements of ANSI/NISO Z39.48-1992 (Permanence of Paper).

Contents

Introduction

This could be the most important day of your life if this is the first you've heard of these wonderful ECK Masters. By the way, "ECK" means the Holy Spirit.

Once you hear of them or perhaps even meet them, you will come to love and respect these wise, able, and compassionate men and women, who remain largely unsung and unheralded in the annals of mankind. They live for one thing and one thing alone: service to God and to all who desperately seek the Lord of Hosts.

Do you count yourself among the true seekers?

Then, there may be a few questions you'd like an answer to. First of all, who are these ECK Masters? What do they do? What about people who've benefited by their help?

And the really big question: What can they do for you?

The purpose of this book is to answer these questions. You'll learn about the wonderful ECK Masters, who they are, and what they've already done for others like you. You'll read the real-life stories of people who've received assistance with health issues, personal concerns, and even finances. Above all, these ECK Masters hold the key to love, wisdom, and spiritual freedom.

So if you love God, love life, and wish to learn more about the ECK Masters—and more about

Do you count yourself among the true seekers?

1

who you really are—please read on. Who knows, you could be at the crossroads of time, on the threshold of new revelations.

You could be on the threshold of new revelations.

May this humble volume shine like a beacon to guide you to God's secret kingdom of love, beauty, and the bounties of joy.

Note: the names of individuals have been changed to safeguard their privacy.

Welcome, now, to the world of those wonderful ECK Masters, who may already be helping you. Read on and see.

Gopal Das (*GOH-pahl DAHS*) was the Mahanta, the Living ECK Master in Egypt, 3000 BC, who founded the mystery cults of Osiris and Isis. He teaches at the Askleposis Temple of Golden Wisdom in the city of Sahasra-dal-Kanwal on the Astral Plane. There, he is the guardian of the holy book of ECK, the Shariyat-Ki-Sugmad.

1
Dream Master
of Ancient Egypt
GOPAL DAS

$\mathcal{M}$any people have been students of one or more ECK Masters in a past lifetime. Others may be surprised to learn of an acquaintanceship with Lai Tsi, Gopal Das, Rebazar Tarzs, or another ECK Master in their dreams. Sometimes dreamers cannot put a name to their dream guide, or they get his name wrong. But the minute they see a picture of the ECK Master, they exclaim in wonder, "Why, he's been my guide for years!"

This connection exists because that ECK Master was the dreamer's beloved guide in some past era.

So numerous people report meeting one or more of the ECK Masters in the dream state. This encounter may also occur during Soul Travel. The mystery of their unknown but ever-resourceful inner companion may go on for years without a resolution, until the individual finally tucks it away in some dusty corner of the mind.

ECK Master Gopal Das is one such dream guide.

The minute they see a picture of the ECK Master, they exclaim in wonder, "Why, he's been my guide for years!"

Who Is Gopal Das?

Gopal Das was the Mahanta, the Living ECK Master in Egypt about 3000 BC when the pharaohs at Saqqara were building pyramids. And it was he who founded the mystery schools of Osiris and Isis. Osiris symbolized the creative forces of nature and the continuity of life, so Gopal Das, the Mahanta, often appeared to early Egyptians in the guise of Osiris. The Mahanta, the Living ECK Master is always the spiritual leader of the ECK followers of his time.

Interest in Gopal Das today arises from his role in dreams as a primary way for one to start his search for the eternal truths that tell of the secrets of God. For you see, it was Gopal Das who inspired the Egyptian book of dreams. It was he who encouraged a scribe in the court of Sesostris III, an Egyptian pharaoh who reigned 1878–1843 BC, to produce it. The Egyptian book of dreams, one of the oldest books known to mankind, contains many dreams and their interpretations. Dreams, then as now, play an important role in the teachings of ECK.

It was Gopal Das who inspired the Egyptian book of dreams.

Our interest in Gopal Das is therefore about his involvement with creative dreaming and the importance of dreams to your spiritual unfoldment.

A rather tall, spare man with light yellow-golden hair, Gopal Das is sometimes mistaken for Christ by people with a Christian background. It is undoubtedly because he often appears in a snow-white robe. Mostly, however, he favors the maroon robe of the Vairagi Order, the brotherhood of the ECK Masters.

A strong interest in spiritual matters such as dreams or prophecy may point to one's earlier training under a Living ECK Master a long time ago.

ECK Masters have quietly existed in society as agriculturists, astronomers, jewelers, painters, businesspeople, and even as sheepherders. They often adopt low-key profiles. In communities where they live, they rub shoulders with ordinary people as well as leaders of society, whose spiritual needs they attend to. It all depends on the mission of each ECK Master.

During Gopal Das's term as the Living ECK Master, the followers of ECK came to suffer much persecution. The orthodox religion and proponents of astrology in Egypt raised such an outcry against the ECK teachings that the Nine Unknown ECK Masters chose to take them underground. It was to be the last time until the modern age that the teachings of the Light and Sound of God would be so available in the public forum.

Of course, the inner dream teachings of ECK never go underground. They are always available. They give instructions vital to all who have no outer way to participate in the spiritual community of ECK. With the outer resources of learning shut down, each chela (spiritual student) nevertheless has an avenue of ECK instruction, a secret link of communication via dreams with the Inner Master. Is it any wonder, then, that many in Eckankar today prize the freedom to belong to an outer spiritual community as one of the great and rare blessings of our times?

A strong interest in spiritual matters such as dreams or prophecy may point to one's earlier training under a Living ECK Master a long time ago.

In the Soul body, Gopal Das made spiritual journeys to teach ECK chelas in North and South America. His students were scattered throughout what is today Canada, the United States, Mexico, Central America, and then on down through South America to the very tip of Cape Horn.

Gopal Das is now guardian of the fourth section of the Shariyat-Ki-Sugmad, the holy book of ECK, on the Astral Plane, in the city of Sahasra-dal-Kanwal. It is at Askleposis, the Golden Wisdom Temple there.

Today, Gopal Das still gives spiritual aid to seekers in every part of the globe, to help them find truth.

Today, he still gives spiritual aid to seekers in every part of the globe, to help them find truth.

Mystery Messenger

The ECK Masters may at times blend events on the Time Track for the benefit of an individual whose destiny it is to find ECK.

One evening, after an ECK introductory talk, a group of people told of how they came to be in Eckankar. Kay Lee told her story:

Way back when she was a senior in high school, she heard mention of Paul Twitchell's book *The Tiger's Fang*. She'd been sitting in the back of the room during a literature class on Dante's *The Divine Comedy*. The discussion was on the first part, which tells of his journey through the regions of hell. Kay Lee was thinking, *Who would want to go through the lower worlds? If I were to make such a journey, I'd rather travel in the higher planes.*

At that moment, a voice spoke from across the room.

"There is a book about the higher worlds," it said. "It's called *The Tiger's Fang.*"

Unaccountably, there came a wonderful feeling of God's love for her. Kay Lee felt an instant liking for the young man who'd spoken, and his strong, yet gentle face. His shoulder-length flaxen hair was light and shining. She didn't remember ever seeing him in class before.

Strangely, no one else showed interest in him or his statement. The instructor, however, shot Kay Lee a disapproving glance for her obvious lack of attention. So she feigned interest in the lecture for a moment before looking back to where the young man had been.

But he was gone!

She enjoyed a clear field of vision right to the door of the classroom and was certain no one had left the room.

The bell rang then, marking the end of class. Though she watched everyone file from the room, the youth with the golden hair was nowhere to be seen. Puzzled, Kay Lee hurried to her next class. Yet the name of that book, *The Tiger's Fang*, remained strongly in her mind. She later learned that the book, written by Paul Twitchell, is an account of his journey into the highest heavens of God. And it was this book that eventually brought her to the teachings of ECK.

Years later, as an ECKist, she finally recognized the mystery man from the classroom as the ECK Master Gopal Das.

But there was more to come. Now some twenty years later, when Kay Lee related her story to the

At that moment, a voice spoke from across the room. "There is a book about the higher worlds," it said.

group after the ECK introductory talk, she got a nudge to check the date of the first printing of *The Tiger's Fang.* It was 1967. That was a full four years after her experience with the blond stranger.

Again came the wonderful feeling of God's great love for her.

Friend, Teacher, Guide, Protector

Marlene was fourteen when she contracted a blood infection that developed into meningitis, an often deadly disease. Critically ill, she fell into a coma and was rushed to a hospital. In the ambulance, amid a flurry of attempts to save her life, Marlene was suddenly out of her body. She stood alongside the stretcher, watching the paramedics struggle to revive her physical self.

Hey! I'm more than my body! was Marlene's first thought. *And I can keep living without it!*

What a happy discovery!

In the twinkling of an eye, Marlene was wrapped in a brilliant blue light. A soothing, humming sound swept through her.

In the twinkling of an eye, Marlene was wrapped in a brilliant blue light. A soothing, humming sound swept through her. A welcome wave of warmth, harmony, and freedom streamed in, more real than anything she'd ever known.

Returning to her physical body, Marlene heard the sound of a monitor recording her vital signs. She was in the intensive-care unit. She could actually hear the rhythmic peeping of the monitor as it broke into the long drawn-out tone of heart failure. How odd to know it was her very own heart.

She left her body a second time but now hovered above it, looking down from a vantage point on the ceiling. For a good while, Marlene observed the doctors working desperately to restore life to her shell of clay. Then, in a flash, she moved upward and away through the roof. Wonderfully there was no pain and no fear.

Seconds later, she stood barefoot on a dew-covered lawn, and from there she could see rolling hills under sunny skies. Marlene knew this as the way home for her. It'd dawned on her that she was *Soul*. Not just a body, but Soul.

It'd dawned on her that she was Soul. *Not just a body, but Soul.*

Then, down from the hills strode a tall, dignified man in a long white robe. Marlene took in his bright blue eyes, shoulder-length blond hair, and beautiful aura. A wave of energy and harmony consumed her. She knew him. Yes, surely, this man was from a past life. Even if she'd never considered the reality of past lives before that moment, she knew he had been her friend, teacher, guide, and protector. He took her hand.

"Let me show you the Kingdom of God," he said, "so you can return to the physical plane refreshed. You must wait until the time is ready to begin your mission."

A while later, Marlene returned to her physical body in the hospital, where doctors predicted a slow recovery for her. It would surely be weeks before she would be well enough to go home. Yet that was the day she began a search for the man she knew to be her guardian angel.

Eighteen years passed. Marlene then had the good fortune to meet an ECKist, the man who would one day become her husband. She found him to be a good listener, so she shared details of her out-of-body experience from childhood. On a hunch, he brought her pictures of the ECK Masters. Marlene was delighted! She recognized her friend and protector, the great ECK Master Gopal Das. Today, Marlene continues her journey home to God through Eckankar. And just as Gopal Das had once foretold, she now discovered her true spiritual mission—to become a Co-worker with God.

But what does that mean?

Co-workers with God

Some may think of Co-worker with God as a rather duty-bound and thus joyless vocation. But those who reach the high states of consciousness find that being a Co-worker with God allows for the most exhilarating opportunity to follow their interests and develop their talents. That explains the joy emanating from the ECK Masters. They all strive to help others—and especially you—reach God-Realization too. And thereby the capacity to give and receive vastly more love.

The ECK Masters all strive to help others—and especially you—reach God-Realization too.

Moreover—and this is important—you can learn to become a Co-worker with God here and now, while still on earth.

The ECK Masters are tried-and-true instruments of divine love. This love for Sugmad (God) fills their hearts and being. They simply must pass it on in wholehearted service to others. For love is life, and life is love. This love pours through them, and there is no way they could contain it even if they wanted to. They are a self-fulfilling law of love.

An act of divine love can be as simple as listening to people tell of the heartaches which have crushed their dreams. And again, it may be in encouraging others to continue their quest to become Co-workers with God. The ECK Masters are the most excellent guides available.

Members of orthodox religions *believe* in the creeds of their faith, but the ECK Masters *know* their relationship with God. Their only creed is God's love.

Soul is a light of God. Sooner or later, It will seek God. What better time is there to get at it than now?

Touched by Love

The road to God is often pitted with loneliness and confusion. Time and patience, though, assure us that we are divine love's own children, for we learn that spiritual help is always there for the asking.

Spiritual help is always there for the asking.

Many years ago, Nancy locked herself in the bathroom with the intention of taking her life. So this youth swallowed an overdose of sleeping pills. She studied her face in the mirror, looking for signs of approaching death. Then, her vision blurred. And gazing back at her in the mirror was the face of a handsome man with blond hair and very blue eyes. Tears welled in them. A single tear fell on his cheek, and with that tear, she sensed a mighty flow of love.

"No," he said, "it's not right to do this."

His sudden appearance jarred her to her senses. She bolted from the bathroom, confessed to her parents what she'd done, and they rushed her to the hospital before harm could be done.

Years later, she recognized her benefactor as the esteemed ECK Master Gopal Das.

She recognized ECK Master Gopal Das. His gaze of love in the mirror had let her glimpse an unknown realm of love and infinite compassion.

His gaze of love in the mirror had let her glimpse an unknown realm of love and infinite compassion. Had she known of it, she would never have risked her precious life. He inspired her to live.

And so, Nancy learned about the healing power of divine love.

The Secrets of ECK

Isaac is an electrical engineer from Africa. He was once called to the home of a retired school principal to perform some electrical work. The principal was well along in years. He mentioned that his father shared his home. As they worked, Isaac told him about ECK. Then, an exceedingly old man entered the room.

"Hey there, what are you doing," he demanded, "telling the secrets of ECK to this child?" The child, of course, was his son.

"They are not secret anymore," said Isaac. "A man named Paul Twitchell made them public in 1965."

The old man pondered over this a minute. Finally, he said, "I first heard about Eckankar in

1914." He went on to describe the ECK Master who'd taken him to a Temple of Golden Wisdom somewhere in the spiritual worlds. "He spoke to me about Eckankar. So, this teaching has finally made it out to the earth plane!"

"What did this Master look like?" asked Isaac.

"He had long blond hair," said the old man.

"I think I know who you mean," said Isaac. "I'll bring you a picture." So he hurried home and found a picture of Gopal Das. The old gentleman recognized him.

"Yes," he affirmed, "that is the man who first told me about the teachings of ECK in 1914."

So Isaac, in going about his livelihood, was able to give news of ECK to two fellow Souls.

The old man said, "He spoke to me about Eckankar. So, this teaching has finally made it out to the earth plane!"

That's Him!

Some time ago, Kara was enjoying a quiet dinner in New York City while visiting two of her grown children. When it came time to leave, they insisted she take a cab home instead of the subway. They even gave her cab fare, so Kara reluctantly agreed.

After giving the cabbie directions, she struck up a conversation with him. It soon turned to spiritual matters. Kara asked if he'd ever had a spiritual experience. He paused a long time before answering.

Then he said, "Well, I keep seeing this guy in my dreams."

"What does he look like?" she asked. The cabbie

gave a detailed description of Gopal Das.

Kara assured him that the appearance of Gopal Das was a spiritual gift. So she told him about Eckankar and the ECK Masters. In the meantime, they'd arrived at her home. He waited patiently while she hurried inside to find a likeness of him. She produced a picture of a handsome man with long golden hair and blue eyes. Was this the cabbie's dream visitor?

The driver put on the interior light to get a better look.

"That's him!" he exclaimed.

The cabbie gave Kara a strange look as if to say, "How the heck do you know someone in my dreams?"

As you may have already guessed, he was gazing at Gopal Das. The cabbie gave Kara a strange look as if to say, "How the heck do you know someone in my dreams?" All in all, he was grateful for the phone number so he could contact Eckankar. Then, he shook Kara's hand.

"Thank you so much," he said. "Thank you so much."

Kara was grateful too. It was a special blessing to help a spiritual seeker find the outer path of ECK. She was learning to become a Co-worker with God and was loving it.

Moving On

Renée was born and raised on a farm in rural Canada. She was the oldest in a large family, which left little time for herself, because Renée's mother needed her help to care for the home and younger children.

Renée, indeed, did all she could, but there

were times her heart cried out for quiet time with God. Then, she'd slip up to her bedroom after dinner, shut the door, then kneel and pray for about half an hour. This brief respite was often interrupted by her mother calling upstairs to ask help with the ironing or some other chores. But the praying made Renée feel good. It relaxed her. She didn't pray for anything special. She just repeated prayers she'd learned as a child in her religion.

Renée well remembers a certain summer evening when she was about sixteen. No one was home but her, a rare occasion. So she used the time to rest and pray. After sunset, she retired to the back porch to gaze at the cloudless sky. To her amazement, a huge cloud began to appear in the west, a human figure clearly visible in the middle of it. It was the image of a man with blond hair and wearing a white robe. He looked at Renée with the most beautiful smile, and a torrent of divine love filled her being. Renée was Catholic, so she assumed it was Jesus.

But why on earth would Jesus appear to me? she wondered. The figure in the cloud began to slowly disappear.

Am I dreaming? Did this really happen?

Renée decided to tell no one, ever, because everyone would think her crazy.

After that, Renée's life carried on with a certain predictability. She married, had children, and remained more or less in the religion of her youth. But in the years to come, there was a shift in her life and in her spiritual needs. She tried to attend

The man with blond hair looked at Renée with the most beautiful smile, and a torrent of divine love filled her being.

church services again, hoping to rekindle her connection with God, but she simply wasn't getting the spiritual food she needed. She always left church still hungry for something more.

One day in church she began to cry. Her tears flowed as if she were a baby, for she felt forsaken and completely alone. Through sob after sob, she asked the Holy Spirit, "Can you help me? I don't feel like I belong here anymore."

An answer came immediately, "You don't belong here anymore. It's OK to leave this church. You must move on."

This was Renée's answer. But where was she to go?

She then began her spiritual search anew and read books on reincarnation. *This really makes sense!* she thought. She'd never explored the subject. In fact, she'd never even heard of reincarnation. Anyway, it was time to open herself to new spiritual ideas.

One day, while watching television, she caught a notice about an Eckankar introductory talk. She fairly leaped from her chair. *That's what I'm looking for!* she thought. So she went to the talk, read an ECK book, and attended a discussion class. She also tried the Spiritual Exercises of ECK suggested in the books and thus began her Soul Travel adventures. Renée had discovered a fresh, new spiritual horizon. Eckankar was the path for her.

Three months later, she came across the portraits of several ECK Masters. One especially caught her eye. It was that of Gopal Das. He was the very

She always left church still hungry for something more.

man who'd appeared in the cloud that summer evening some thirty years ago.

Renée now begins every single day with heart-felt thanks to the ECK, the Holy Spirit, for putting her spiritual life in order.

Gift of a Kitten

Sometimes it is a love for something outside yourself that opens you to the presence of the ECK Masters. What you give to another of God's creatures will return to you as a blessing, through the grace of the divine ECK. Gloria's story is an example of this.

Gloria was in ECK sixteen years. Along the way, she'd acquired a beautiful Siamese kitten for her family from the Animal Rescue League. The first four days of romping with this new member of the household brought her a realization: this would be an indoor cat, so her front claws would have to go. But Gloria felt guilty about taking the kitten to a vet to be declawed. So she sat down with the kitten in her lap and did a spiritual exercise.

She asked for guidance. Was it OK to go ahead with the declawing procedure?

In contemplation, she saw a tunnel of swirling white light, and then ECK Master Gopal Das stood before her. He said the kitten knew and had agreed to it, knowing that to live in this family meant having to be declawed.

"Don't worry," he said. "She understands and has agreed to this."

Sometimes it is a love for something outside yourself that opens you to the presence of the ECK Masters.

Gloria felt much better then. She realized that in all her years of being in ECK, it was her first face-to-face meeting with Gopal Das.

This was the gift that came with her Siamese kitten.

A Good Start

Sandra is the young mother of two, a four-year old boy and a girl of about fifteen months. She reads to them from *The ECK Teensie Discourses,* a book with stories, games, and activities to help children learn the ways of ECK. Her son is profoundly handicapped. She feels that if he learns nothing more than divine love, he has learned the most important thing of all. He is also deaf. The family must often use sign language to communicate with him.

One day, Sandra was reading to her daughter, Bethany, when they came to a page with pictures of the ECK Masters. Right away Bethany pointed to a drawing of today's Living ECK Master. She knew him.

Sandra asked, "Do you know anyone else here?"

The toddler quickly pointed to a drawing of Gopal Das. "Gopal," she said.

It must be said that Sandra had never spoken to Bethany about Gopal Das, but it was clear that they knew each other. Bethany's casual revelation left Sandra bemused. So she asked if Bethany knew any of the ECK Masters on some other drawings.

In sign language picked up from the family,

The toddler quickly pointed to a drawing of Gopal Das. "Gopal," she said. It was clear they knew each other.

Bethany said, "All done. No more." The little teacher was done teaching for now.

Before Bethany's birth, Sandra dreamed she saw a little girl peeking from behind the legs of the Living ECK Master, who introduced Sandra as her mother-to-be. It was a sure sign they'd been together before this life.

Sandra looks forward to a strong spiritual bond with her daughter in this lifetime.

Dream Portrait

An upswing in one's spiritual unfoldment may already begin weeks or months before he finally reaches the decision to come into Eckankar. And it's due to an ECK Master in some unrecognized way. The ECK Master will accompany him to certain holy places in the spiritual worlds. The dreamer may remember what happened there.

The ECK Master will accompany him to certain holy places in the spiritual worlds.

Yuko is a Japanese woman who recently became a member of Eckankar. She reported the following dream:

She was riding on a bus with other passengers and informed the driver of wanting to get off at a certain stop.

"That's a very dangerous place at night," he cautioned her. "You don't want to get off there by yourself."

"I'll go with you," a male passenger offered.

So Yuko, as well as a small number of other passengers, alighted from the bus and were met by a woman, a child, and several others. The moon smiled in the dark sky as this little group headed down a road.

The road crossed a path that led to a house nestled high in the mountains. The man from the bus pushed open the glass door, and all trooped inside. On a wall hung a picture of a fellow with long golden hair.

"Who's that?" asked Yuko.

"You remember, don't you?" the man from the bus said.

Then she did. She'd reached this very same mountain home so many times before, on the very same bus. Yuko also recognized the man in the picture, who'd always accompanied her. The dream ended. But she retained a crystal clear memory of the setting and the man.

Soon after, Yuko attended an ECK Satsang (study) class. There, displayed on a table as part of the class discussion, were sketches of four ECK Masters. She threw them a careless glance. One, however, made her look again.

Gopal Das and other ECK Masters guide dream travelers to these rest points in eternity.

"He's the same man I saw in the picture in my dream!" she exclaimed, pointing to one of the sketches.

And who do you suppose that mystery man was?

Yes, the ECK Master Gopal Das.

He and other ECK Masters guide dream travelers such as Yuko to these rest points in eternity. It helps people get used to the ways of the other worlds, sometimes long before they're ready for the true teaching of ECK outwardly.

A Spiritual Exercise to Meet Gopal Das

Would you like to meet an ECK Master on your own initiative?

Chances are, you already have. But a prudish censor of the mind can decide which experiences might cause you to become an unbalanced nuisance to society. Consequently, it may erase or distort your memory of what it deems a threatening inner experience. However, there is a way to meet the great ECK Master Gopal Das anyway. Try this exercise:

First, sit in an easy chair with your eyes shut. Then imagine yourself in a warm, dry climate where the air is sweet and fresh, and where everything in sight is of a pleasing golden color. Only the sky is all blue.

Finally, sing the word *Gopal* (GOH-pahl) in two syllables, with the accent on the first. Sing it for ten minutes or more with a clear mind. In a wink, you may suddenly be in a high spiritual world with Gopal Das or another ECK Master. You will be taken to a Temple of Golden Wisdom or some other fascinating location.

It may take a bit to catch on to the simplicity of this spiritual exercise, but do stay with it. Patience and determination go a long way toward success. Then you, too, will meet such wonderful spiritual travelers as Gopal Das.

In a wink, you may suddenly be in a high spiritual world with Gopal Das or another ECK Master.

Fubbi Quantz (*FOO-bee KWAHNTS*) was the Mahanta, the Living ECK Master during the time of Buddha, about 500 BC. He completed his mission, then immortalized his body, and is now the guardian of the Shariyat-Ki-Sugmad at the Katsupari Monastery in northern Tibet.

2
Abbot of
the Katsupari Monastery
FUBBI QUANTZ

*W*ho are the ECK Masters?

A Co-worker with God means the highest spiritual consciousness embodied in individuals we call ECK Masters.

These ECK Masters go unknown among the people. Except for the few Masters whose job it is to work in the public eye, they rarely, if ever, speak about who they are. Titles are of small interest to them. What does matter, however, is giving upliftment to Soul—to even one lone Soul somewhere. If they can do this for even one, that's all the reward they need.

The ECK Masters walk among you now, today, ready to encourage one Soul at a time on the journey home to God.

The ECK Masters walk among you today, ready to encourage one Soul at a time on the journey home to God.

Abbot of the Katsupari Monastery

Fubbi Quantz is the abbot of the Katsupari Monastery in the Buika Magna Mountains of northern Tibet.

This monastery is near the Valley of Shangta,

gathering place for the ECK Masters at the passing of the Rod of ECK Power. Legend had it that Jesus once went there during his "silent years" and met the ECK Abbot Fubbi Quantz, reputed to be of a remarkable age in the same body.

Chief among the writings in the Katsupari Monastery is the first section of the Shariyat-Ki-Sugmad, "The Chronicles of ECK." The Kadath Inscriptions, also found there, provide a historical record of the Living ECK Masters throughout the ages. The Records of the Kros, another set of old documents, relate the history of earth and prophesy its future.

Years before the Chinese invasion of Tibet, intrepid travelers came to Katsupari for the Kaya Kalp treatments of physical rejuvenation. The Oracle of Tirmer is nearby.

Who Is Fubbi Quantz?

Fubbi Quantz is a tall, elderly man with white hair and beard, and a gentle smile. Good humor gleams in his eyes.

Fubbi Quantz teaches from the sacred scriptures of the Shariyat-Ki-Sugmad, the holy book of ECK. Many students come to him in the dream state to study when they first begin on the path of Eckankar.

He is a tall, elderly man with white hair and beard, and a gentle smile. Good humor gleams in his eyes. Paul Twitchell once described him as having a lantern jaw, and the description fits. Usually Fubbi appears to spiritual students in a white robe that reaches well below the knees. All who may attend his classes on the Shariyat are fortunate indeed, for he passes on the Light and

Music of God to all who are there.

Fubbi Quantz once served as the Mahanta, the Living ECK Master. This was during the time of Buddha, around the sixth century BC. After completing his mission, he immortalized his body and continues to serve the spiritual needs of mankind. He later served as teacher of Firdusi, the Persian poet, and was also the spiritual guide of Columbus. It was Fubbi Quantz who inspired Columbus to sail to the Americas, to open the vast storehouse of new sorely needed sources of fruits, grains, legumes, vegetables, and especially protein there.

It was Fubbi Quantz who inspired Columbus to sail to the Americas.

It was then the late fifteenth century. In his travels around Europe, Fubbi Quantz had witnessed the appalling health of the European people. It was in a shocking state. They had little energy left over after a day's work for contemplation or reflection, the moment of quiet which is the sweet drink of Soul. So Fubbi Quantz gave Columbus a vision one night. In it he showed the potential of the New World. This vision fired the imagination of Columbus and thus set into motion the events that led him to sail his three tiny ships westward into unknown waters. In the Americas, then, European explorers found both precious minerals and abundant stores of life-giving foods. Thus, Fubbi Quantz revived the food stock and nutrition of the Old World.

Fubbi Quantz had a deep yearning to find God even as a young man. But before it was possible for him to do so, he first had to go through the mystic rites of fire and water. It is a secret initiation in which much old karma is burned off and washed away. It is a major turning point in one's spiritual evolution. And it comes only through ECK (Holy Spirit).

What preparatory steps were involved that carried him even beyond that stage so he could enter the circle of ECK Adepts and Vairagi Masters?

He was studying at a monastery then, and life had put him where he couldn't see a way out to find spiritual freedom. So he made the decision to climb a holy mountain in search of enlightenment. He supposed that such a mountain peak was as good a place as any to continue his quest. When he reached the summit, he cried, "God, why have you forsaken me?"

After a while there came a voice. It said, "My son, I haven't forsaken you. I've been with you through the ages." And the lightning flashed, and thunder rolled.

A voice said, "My son, I haven't forsaken you. I've been with you through the ages."

From that day on, Fubbi Quantz knew the true meaning of the ancient promise of the Mahanta, the Living ECK Master: "I am always with you." That promise still resounds today. The current Master gives that same assurance to all ECK followers now, even as have the ECK Masters of old.

Fubbi Quantz then had the experience of God (Sugmad). He has been to the Anami, the Ocean of Love and Mercy, many times since.

After this experience of God-Realization, he returned to the monastery. The abbot in charge knew and understood what experience he'd had and so left him alone. Fubbi Quantz retired to his cell and contemplated for a long time. Later, he came out and took up his mission. He was to become the Mahanta, the Living ECK Master of those times.

Now, would you like to read of his spiritual help to people in search of truth?

Agents of God

After her grandmother died, Shelley had trouble falling asleep at night.

Sleep came hard because now a fear of death had locked an iron grip on her. She'd once been a follower of the teachings of ECK but had since lost her early connection with them. So she forgot about singing HU, the ancient love song to God, which offers comfort and spiritual protection when all else fails. Still, she had grown up in an ECK family. And so there remained a golden thread to the teachings of ECK from that early exposure years ago. Shelley thus benefited from the protection of the ECK Masters.

These agents of God work in a special way with people for whom they feel an affinity or friendship.

These agents of God work in a special way with people for whom they feel an affinity.

So at night, while tossing and turning and trying to sleep, she often caught sight of an old man in her Spiritual Eye. Long white hair graced his head; his eyes were like deep pools of love and compassion. Each time he entered her room, the dreadful fear would vanish so she could sleep. This happened time and again. At length, the fear of death lost its sting, and she was able to get on with life.

One day, Shelley stopped at her mother's home. ECK books were on a bookshelf, and pictures of the ECK Masters decorating a wall caught her attention.

"That's the same man who came to my room when I couldn't sleep," she said to her mom. She indicated the picture of ECK Master Fubbi Quantz, who had served as the spiritual leader of ECK in days long ago.

Even though an ECK Master may have retired from that position, a special bond of love still exists between him and his former disciples. And he continues to lend a helping hand to them on their journey home to God. These people may have left the teachings of ECK; even so, the love and protection of their former Master remains with them. This love and protection is always there in times of great need.

The guardian angels we hear of in the media are often ECK Masters.

That is exactly what Shelley learned.

Guardian Angels

The guardian angels we hear of in the media are often ECK Masters. The ECK Masters are guardian angels. However, not all guardian angels are ECK Masters, and there's a real difference.

A guardian angel's main role is to protect people. Such a guardian picks a person and stays with him, to provide help with whatever powers lie in that guardian's keeping. But different angels have different levels of ability. Look at students in a classroom: they are not equal and alike in their abilities. The same is true of angels.

Spiritual Freedom

Maria, from Mexico, met the ECK Master Fubbi Quantz seven years before she ever heard of the ECK teachings.

At the time she worked in a store in Mexico City. It was a good store, and she liked the owners, who sold valuable art, paintings, and old books.

Maria had planned to take off from work for forty-five days to travel to Europe with her husband. But it meant leaving her little girls at home. As she considered this situation, Maria felt a strong reluctance to go on the vacation.

When he spoke, the words flowing from his mouth were like priceless pearls of wisdom.

One day, near the departure date, an old man entered the shop. He looked like a native of India, yet he addressed her in perfect English.

Another of the sales clerks said to Maria, "You speak English. Would you like to help him?" So Maria approached the man with a warm and friendly smile.

While they talked, she was struck by his genuine kindness. He was so very kind and courteous. And when he spoke, the words flowing from his mouth were more than casual, ordinary ones, for they were like priceless pearls of wisdom. Each shone with an unmistakable luminescence.

Their conversation lasted for some time. At length he said, "You're always smiling, but why are your eyes so sad?"

She said, "I think maybe it's because I don't

have freedom inside myself. I have freedom out here, but I don't have it inside."

He said, "Ah, yes. Spiritual freedom. You want spiritual freedom."

The Secret of Love

What did he mean by spiritual freedom? As if reading her thoughts, the old man pulled a coin from his pocket and showed it to her. On the coin was a face.

"Look carefully at this silver coin," he said. "See the face on it?" Maria studied the face.

"The person on the face of this coin is trying to lead people to spiritual freedom," the old gentleman continued. "I would like you to have this coin."

"I can't just take your coin," she said.

He persisted. "Please, take it," he said. "It will always remind you of spiritual freedom."

Finally she took it. Soon after, she and her husband began their trip to Europe. First stop was Spain. They also decided on a quick side trip to Italy, where Maria got a strong sense of déjà vu. Had she ever lived there in a past life? Things were very familiar. Too familiar to be a coincidence.

And in the quiet alcoves of her mind there lingered the matter of the silver coin. What had the old man in the shop meant by spiritual freedom?

Yet not until seven years later did Maria encounter the teachings of ECK. It happened like this:

During a visit to a local ECK center, she saw

drawings of the ECK Masters. One was of the ECK Master Fubbi Quantz. Why, that was the very gentleman she'd met in the store! Looking at the drawing, Maria felt an overwhelming wave of love and gratitude sweep over her. She'd found the secret of love! The secret lay in the teachings of ECK, for it was ECK Master Fubbi Quantz who'd introduced the fountain of divine love into her life.

Maria had spent her entire life searching for divine love. And until she'd found the ECK teachings, life was like a stagnant pool, without a brook to feed it. She'd carried a sense of deep sadness for years without any idea of where to search for spiritual freedom, and Fubbi Quantz had read its absence in her eyes.

But now, there was finally the light of joy.

Memory of Stars

Sarah, a Nigerian, first heard of Eckankar on a recording of a televised talk I'd given some years earlier.

Sarah had caught the last segment of a three-part program introducing the ECK teachings. To her utter amazement, a perfect six-pointed blue star replaced my face on the TV screen. She recognized it as a spiritual gift, and it was a great inspiration to her. And so she drove to an ECK center to borrow ECK books. It was there that she noticed an event taking place in the next room. The center's host invited her to stay and attend the event, which happened to be an ECK Worship Service.

Maria felt an overwhelming wave of love and gratitude sweep over her. She'd found the secret of love!

In the room used for the service, Sarah noticed pictures of the ECK Masters. Right off, one of the pictures drew her fascinated attention. This is her story:

Some six years earlier, Sarah had suffered grave injuries in a car accident, which left her unconscious for four days. She showed no response whatever to medical treatments, so the doctors decided to disconnect her life-support system.

At that very critical moment, an old man came to her on the inner planes. He told her to ask the doctors for a bed next to the wall.

Sarah stirred from the unconscious state and made the request. No sooner had the staff moved her to the new location than she slipped into a quite normal sleep. But this applied only to her physical body. In a subtle, inner body she awoke under a wondrous and most beautiful covering of silvery stars. Dancing, sparkling lights covered her bed and the walls.

Ever since that experience, Sarah felt a deep longing of some kind in her heart.

Ever since that experience, Sarah felt a deep longing of some kind in her heart. But a longing for what, she couldn't say.

In the days and weeks to come, Sarah showed a remarkable recovery. Her doctor warned she'd carry severe deformities from her injuries, yet in six months all her bones had healed, much to her doctor's surprise.

So it was on that day in the ECK center that Sarah chanced upon the picture of a certain ECK Master. To her surprise and delight, she learned the identity of the old man who'd come to her in the hospital a full six years earlier. It was none other than the venerable Fubbi Quantz. His picture was the final, long awaited sign that her spiritual seeking had reached an end.

The ECK teachings were like a cool, healing salve to Sarah's once-restless, seeking heart.

Appointment with Truth

Many who embrace the ECK teachings today have in one way or another had spiritual experiences that most people have not. Counted among them may be such things as near-death experiences, out-of-the-body adventures, or remarkable dreams and visions.

In most cases, though, it's better that people not have such experiences day in and day out. They may find themselves unable to handle them. So they spin out of control, losing a necessary balance. This makes a lot of trouble for everyone.

Dramatic psychic or spiritual experiences often catch people leaning. This usually happens before they come to Eckankar. But such experiences do serve to awaken them spiritually. With a sense of wonder and self-doubt, they may well ask, *What happened? Am I losing my mind?* So they turn to some authority to find an answer to their unusual experience. "So what happened to me?" they say. The minister shrugs his shoulders. Doctors of philosophy, psychology, or one of the medical arts return blank looks.

Where to now?

On that day she learned the identity of the old man who'd come to her in the hospital six years earlier.

Let's follow Terry and watch how he went about finding the answer to a spiritual question that had troubled him.

Terry began his spiritual search with a simple expression of gratitude. During a spiritual exercise, he had been filled with the wonder of God, grateful for life and the love of his family.

Then, unexpectedly, a life-changing event occurred in contemplation.

He had a vision! Time seemed to stand still. The darkness parted and there appeared a spiritual being clothed in a radiant white light. Terry took him to be Jesus. In time, however, he learned it was none other than the great ECK Master Fubbi Quantz.

Nothing like this had ever happened to him. He felt both blessed and startled by the vision. He wanted answers. What was the overwhelming love he felt for this man? What did the vision mean? And so he went to his pastor.

Terry told of his vision of the spiritual being in a white light. Who was he? Maybe the pastor could help him understand this unsettling experience with the unknown. But his pastor shrugged his shoulders. Instead, he offered Terry the story of what had once happened to him.

It was also a life-changing experience.

Many years earlier he had been an ordinary student at a university. While heading across campus, he felt a hand on his shoulder. It spun him around ninety degrees to face him toward the theology building. Yet there was no one around. Who could have spun him around? The student

Terry began his spiritual search with an expression of gratitude. Then, unexpectedly, a life-changing event occurred in contemplation.

took this as a sign to change his career. So he walked directly to the theology building and enrolled in the ministerial program. Here, a lifetime later, he was ministering to others. Yet he still remained curious about the encounter that forever marked a change in his life.

Terry realized something then. His old religion could no longer offer him the food he needed to satisfy his spiritual longing.

What did Terry's vision mean? He still didn't know. Apart from sharing his own experience, his pastor was no closer to knowing the reason for it than Terry was to his.

So Terry began to research spiritual topics. Each step he took brought him closer to finding his path.

His old religion could no longer offer him the food he needed to satisfy his spiritual longing.

Then one day, Terry heard a remarkable thing about a man who worked at the same job site, where heavy-water processing plants were built. There was an employee who spent his lunch hour atop one of the site's five-hundred-foot towers. There, rumor had it he went "flying off to the inner worlds." A friend reported this to Terry.

His friend was befuddled by the story, but Terry had a strong feeling it was a lead in his search for spiritual truth.

So he made it a point to meet that employee. The man, he learned, was an ECKist, who gave him *In My Soul I Am Free* by Brad Steiger. Now out of print, it was a biography of Paul Twitchell, the modern-day founder of Eckankar.

Terry had found exactly what he was looking

for. The teachings resonated within him. Soon he and his wife became members, and his spiritual life blossomed with the richness of the Light and Sound of ECK.

No longer was Terry shopping for truth. Answers to his spiritual questions began to appear. He also discovered the identity of the man in his vision, the headwaters of his spiritual quest. It was the ECK Master Fubbi Quantz. It was he who had come to Terry years earlier in that vision, stirring the energies of Soul, to set out and learn his spiritual destiny.

And so, indeed, he had.

Every person has a chance to learn of spiritual freedom. The ECK Masters light up an event, a dream, or an unusual encounter to clear the way.

Dream Awakening

Every person has a chance to learn of spiritual freedom. The ECK Masters light up an event, a dream, or an unusual encounter to clear the way for an individual to recognize God's love call for Soul to come home.

Many long years ago, Travis came across *ECKANKAR—The Key to Secret Worlds* by Paul Twitchell. The young man was enthralled. The book felt so "right." As a result, Travis stayed up all night to read it.

In due time, he had a dream with an ECK Master whose identity he later learned was Fubbi Quantz. In the dream, Travis felt himself falling, as if into a deep well. But he was, in fact, returning from the higher worlds to reenter his sleeping, human body. As he fell and landed in his own bed again, a book had tumbled along after him. Its title was *In My Soul I Am Free.*

Travis could not remember anything that Fubbi Quantz had said; he only remembered Fubbi's face. But upon awakening, he felt a very distinct change inside him.

Later that day he went to the bookstore where he worked. Once there, he noticed a new book display on a table. The store had just set out *In My Soul I Am Free,* the story of Paul Twitchell and Eckankar. This was the book from his dream! In that selfsame moment, Travis realized that Eckankar was for him, and he for it.

In the months and years to come, he would discover what the message from Fubbi Quantz had been that night. Fubbi had given Travis assurance that the teachings of ECK were the spiritual food he needed to make it through the tumblings of his life.

And so it was that Travis met Fubbi Quantz and discovered the secret doctrines of Eckankar.

Travis only remembered Fubbi's face. But upon awakening, he felt a very distinct change inside him.

Trail Guide

An article once ran in the *San Jose Mercury,* a West Coast newspaper, that carried the intriguing title "A Bike Ride Stranger than Fiction."

Twin brothers decided to take their mountain bikes to one of the large parks in California. They planned to make a forty-mile loop along ridges and up and down trails to see if they could reach a certain summit.

So they stopped at a ranger station to leave their itinerary. A ranger said matter-of-factly, "If your truck is still parked out here by our station in the morning, we'll come looking for you."

Was this a foreshadowing of what they might expect? This park is in a remote and wild location. Coyotes, wild boar, cougars, hawks, and other creatures still roam there. In the dark areas of its forest lies a good deal of danger.

Was this a foreshadowing of what they might expect?

So the two young men, full of adventure, set out on their bikes to rough it, racing up and down hills and ravines. After a while, they were exhausted.

One asked, "Will we be able to make the summit and still get back to the ranger station before dark?"

This ride was turning out to be a lot more strenuous than they'd bargained for. Yet, in spite of extreme tiredness, they decided to push on. Before long they managed to reach the summit.

Both exclaimed in wonder, "Wow, what a view!" Then more soberly, one said, "Now we'd better get on out of here."

Off in the distance at the next ridge, they could see a rainstorm sweeping in. Trouble. Rain would turn the trails to mud. When the rainstorm unleashed its vengeance, biking went from bad to worse. The trail had indeed turned to mud. They drove themselves without mercy, to the point of thinking it was the end. The brothers struggled on. Finally, they collapsed.

They'd toppled into the mud—flat on their backs, unable to stir a muscle. The danger of exposure was all too real. One concluded, "Well, it's been a good life." So they lay there, in the mud, exchanging stories of adventures they'd shared in their all-too-short lives.

Suddenly, an old man appeared before them. He had a walking stick in hand, and wore an old rain cap on his head. But his most striking feature was a long white beard.

The man studied them. Finally, he asked, "What are you doing?"

The twins answered in unison, as twins often do. "We're going to die," they said. It was said mostly in jest, but in truth they felt it might well turn out to be the case. They'd likely reached the end of the line. The two peered up at the old gentleman miserably.

Finally, one said, "Where'd you come from?" Still on their bed of mud, flat on their backs, they looked up, too worn out to budge.

Brushing the question aside, he stated, "I am a caretaker."

"Where's the trail back to the ranger station?" they asked.

His eyes reflected a gentle, compassionate look. "That's the way home," he said, pointing to a place hidden beyond trailside brush. Indeed, just a few yards away, was the elusive trail they'd sought. The old man regarded them with amusement. "So you guys aren't ready to die." His gentle humor was like a healing tonic.

The old man regarded them with amusement. "So you guys aren't ready to die."

Unaccountably refreshed, they roused, straddled their bikes, and headed for the trailhead a few yards away. They stopped and turned to wave their gratitude to the old gentleman, but he had vanished.

The two young men reached the ranger station, starved. One of them, the writer of the newspaper article, made straight for a fast-food restaurant to order three large hamburgers and fries. In ecstasy, he savored his gourmet meal. Then he cleaned up in the washroom, rinsed off the mud, and headed home to a soft, warm bed.

There was an odd follow-up to their adventure. The writer of the article told of a later dream in which the old caretaker appeared to him. The young man asked, "What are you doing in my dream?"

The old one replied, "I came to say that you have more adventures ahead of you and to be thankful."

"Thankful for what?"

"You are a wild spirit and have a big heart." Smiling, he added, "Be thankful for every minute you are here."

The young man shot back, "You mean wander the hills alone like you?"

"No. Be the caretaker of your life."

When the dreamer awoke, contentment and happiness hovered over him such as he'd not felt for a long time. His conclusion from this dream was that we are all caretakers for ourselves and each other, and it's important to take every step with grace. For life is a precious journey.

"And most of all," the young writer urged, "Don't ever give up."

Most ECKists will recognize the old man in this story is the ECK Master Fubbi Quantz.

The young man asked, "What are you doing in my dream?"

In the Grasp of Divine Love

Sherry, a businesswoman, once tried a Spiritual Exercise of ECK and was fortunate to meet the revered ECK Master Fubbi Quantz at the Katsupari Monastery. The location of this monastery is indeed on the physical plane, yet it lies hidden from human eyes. A real place, it is well hidden to protect it from all who would seek its destruction.

There, Fubbi Quantz took Sherry into a room for a spiritual healing.

The room is round. Some of you reading this have been there too. The domed ceiling is supported by struts that soar heavenward. There is a cot that looks as if it might provide a hard and uncomfortable rest, yet a patient finds it surprisingly comfortable. When a patient like Sherry lies upon the cot, the Light and Sound of God bathes the individual with Its healing and restorative powers.

When a patient lies upon the cot, the Light and Sound of God bathes the individual with Its healing and restorative powers.

Such was Sherry's experience. When she arose from the cot, she felt renewed and much, much stronger in body and spirit.

Her thoughts then turned to the future course of her life.

Fubbi Quantz said, "The ECK has you firmly in the grasp of divine love. So, no need to worry. A perfect design is woven, and you are a strand in it. Be quiet and purposeful in this phase of your life." It was the exact answer Sherry had been hoping for.

And, of course, it'd come as a direct result of

doing the Spiritual Exercises of ECK, as had her spiritual healing. Everything was a gift of love to Sherry from the wonderful ECK Master Fubbi Quantz.

Heaven for You

The ECK Masters help all who really want to find the true love and wisdom that is their divine heritage.

The ECK Masters enjoy the highest states of consciousness. They live in the high heavens and are prepared to help all who really want to find the true love and wisdom that is their divine heritage.

The first goal for such a seeker is Self-Realization. He quickly learns he must have the help of the Mahanta, the Living ECK Master to attain the true love and wisdom he seeks. At length, each Soul will unfold into the fullness of God Consciousness itself. But this requires changes in him. It means developing certain virtues by way of certain disciplines. We know these disciplines as the Spiritual Exercises of ECK.

Where and how are the exercises to be done?

You may do these spiritual exercises at home, in private. No one else need know. Only you will know of your successes or missteps on the road to God.

Only you and the Inner Master need ever know.

⭒ A Spiritual Exercise to Meet Fubbi Quantz

Reread the description of the round room of healing in the Katsupari Monastery from "In the Grasp of Divine Love" a few pages ago.

Now sing HU, the ancient love song to God. Pronounce it like the common word *hue*. Sing it softly with shut eyes, and try to imagine the large round room and its vaulted ceiling. What is the color of the room, its furniture, if any? At the same time, try to feel the soothing currents of the Light and Sound of God move in gentle and majestic rhythms through the room while you are resting upon the cot of healing.

You may also ask Fubbi Quantz a question should you wish to do so. The answer will often come later, after you've finished your contemplation and have returned to the waking state. It may appear while reading *The Shariyat-Ki-Sugmad*, the ECK holy book. The answer may likewise come to light through the Golden-tongued Wisdom, a seemingly random thought that jumps out at you from the words of some person. You may also hear Fubbi Quantz's gentle voice whisper the answer in your ear.

Listen. Be aware until it comes. For it surely will.

You may ask Fubbi Quantz a question. The answer may come through the Golden-tongued Wisdom.

Lai Tsi (*lie TSEE*) is the Chinese ECK Master who is the guardian of the Shariyat-Ki-Sugmad on the Saguna Lok, the Etheric Plane, at the Temple of Golden Wisdom in the city of Arhirit. He once served as the Mahanta, the Living ECK Master.

3
Chinese Sage of Wisdom
LAI TSI

*O*ccasionally, I get letters from people who are not members of Eckankar. Some of them are already receiving the ECK teachings on the inner planes, and it surprises them to learn their teacher is an ECK Master.

Ellen wrote to me from Florida. Although she's not an ECKist, a friend of hers is. Ellen has at certain times made comments to which her friend would reply, "Why, that's straight from *The Shariyat.*" *The Shariyat-Ki-Sugmad* is the bible of Eckankar and means "Way of the Eternal." It has always amazed her ECKist friend when Ellen comes up with echoes of philosophies and statements straight from *The Shariyat.*

Finally, Ellen became curious about *The Shariyat.* What was it? She'd read a few ECK books, but not *The Shariyat.* So she began to read it.

Not long thereafter came a dream.

Ellen Learns Her Spiritual Mission

In this dream, someone drove Ellen to a distant meeting place where a number of people had gathered. Among them was the Mahanta, the

Living ECK Master. He approached her and revealed a bit of her mission in this lifetime. She had long felt that such a mission did exist, but how was it to play out?

The next morning, this dream with the Mahanta remained set in her mind. Others might regard it as little more than an ordinary dream, but to her it went far beyond that.

Shortly after this, Ellen sat in meditation when a small Chinese man appeared unexpectedly in her inner vision. He was dressed in western-style clothing, all in blue from head to toe. Unknown to her, it was the beloved ECK Master Lai Tsi, whose blue clothing switched to a maroon robe in the blink of an eye. On his head perched a happy but odd little red cap, while he danced and laughed with joyful abandon. At seeing him, Ellen felt an enormous sense of joy and goodwill in her heart.

She wondered, How can this little man have such power to bring so much happiness to me?

She wondered, *How can this little man have such power to bring so much happiness to me?*

The realization Ellen gained from her two inner experiences was that she is to serve as an instrument for divine love. That is her mission. And as she pursues the ECK teachings, a fuller understanding about this mission of love will come to her. She'll learn a right understanding of it. But in the end, Ellen's overall mission is simply to become a Co-worker with God.

The only reason Soul exists is because God loves It. One who recognizes this principle will find countless ways to give divine love to all life— to all creatures and beings.

Ellen will learn this in due time. Indeed, all

Souls will learn this. It's just a matter of time.

Temple of Dayaka

Lai Tsi serves as the guardian of a section of the Shariyat-Ki-Sugmad on the Etheric Plane. A dream traveler will find the Shariyat housed in the Temple of Dayaka, in the city of Arhirit.

Now imagine if you can, a huge round temple more than a hundred stories to the top of its spire. Windows encircle the structure. A shining golden ball rests on top of the spire, and its brilliance is greater than that of our sun or any other sun in our universe. Its rays reach out to the very edges of the Etheric Plane.

The Shariyat-Ki-Sugmad itself rests on a lectern hundreds of feet below this golden ball of radiant light.

Lai Tsi is a slender man of medium height and usually wears his hair in a single braid to his shoulders. Luminous dark eyes and a wide and smiling mouth speak of benevolence and goodwill. He may appear to seekers as a silver light, along with a humming sound like that of buzzing bees. Other people besides Ellen have reported seeing him in a maroon robe, but wearing a high, brimless hat, whose ornaments and symbols are of a mysterious and unknown origin.

Lai Tsi may appear to seekers as a silver light, along with a humming sound like buzzing bees.

Who's That Master?

In Johannesburg, South Africa, there lives an ECKist who writes computer programs for a living. Douglas once developed a computer program for a fair in Johannesburg, a program about the ECK teachings to catch the eye of passersby. One of its segments showed portraits of ECK Masters, who appeared on the screen in sequence.

Children loved his presentation. The animated scenes and images of the ECK Masters fascinated them.

A young woman stopped at the booth and asked, "Who's that Chinese Master?"

Douglas said it was Lai Tsi.

"Every time I've come past your booth, this Master happens to be on the screen," she said. "He's been my guide here in my life, and I just wondered who he was. I didn't know his name."

This led to a discussion about the ECK Master Lai Tsi and the ECK teachings.

For the most part, Lai Tsi's work is now on the inner planes. He helps people who were his students in past lifetimes, to prepare them for the path of Eckankar today. This woman was one of them. Her spiritual destiny was truly in the hands of divine love, and Douglas's computer program had piqued her interest. It marked a turning point in her spiritual affairs.

Douglas's love for programming thus became an instrument for Divine Spirit to reach her. And all this happened because of his desire to give people at the fair a new and novel look at the ECK Masters.

She said, "He's been my guide here in my life, and I wondered who he was. I didn't know his name."

Who Is Lai Tsi?

As a young man Lai Tsi was one of many monks who studied religion in the schools of ancient China. He later became a revered doctor of divinity. But at some point, he understood that the realization of God could never be gained from books. He thus determined to look for it in the solitude and stillness of nature.

So Lai Tsi left society and set off to live in a cave high in the mountains above the Yellow River (Huang) in north central China.

There, two ECK Masters began to call on him. One was Tomo Geshig. This Master came to visit in the Soul body for seven years before they ever met in the flesh. Tomo Geshig was a wanderer. He roamed the Himalaya alone, dressed in old robes. A lesser mortal would surely have perished in the unrelenting cold.

This Master came to visit in the Soul body for seven years before they ever met in the flesh.

The other ECK Master who came in the Soul body to teach Lai Tsi was Yaubl Sacabi, and his age is beyond human comprehension. He, like Tomo Geshig, came to Lai Tsi to give words of love and inspiration about Sugmad (God) and Its creation.

The spiritual instruction from these two ECK Masters paid off in a big way.

The day came that Lai Tsi was lifted out of his physical body into the high worlds of God, where he experienced the Light and Sound of God in a most wonderful and memorable way. There, far beyond the reaches of time and space, he beheld the Sugmad, Lord of all Lords. Yet when Lai Tsi returned to his physical body three days later, he couldn't describe a single feature of the Sugmad.

And while his body had lain unconscious the whole time of his heavenward journey, Lai Tsi lived despite the cold. His spell of unconsciousness had lasted three days. He survived because the Sugmad had urged the animals and birds of the mountains to care for him, to ensure his survival.

When Lai Tsi awoke from his journey to God, he lay on the chill floor of the cave. While he'd been out of his body, in the ecstatic state, a lion had cooled his fevered brow with its tongue. Wild deer had snuggled close to provide warmth against the freezing air.

It seemed as if all of life, all of nature, had the single purpose of making certain his survival.

Then too, when Lai Tsi finally opened his eyes, he saw Tomo Geshig busy in front of a roaring blaze, preparing food to nurture and restore him.

Lai Tsi's Mission

Lai Tsi had become the Living ECK Master. His new state of consciousness soared far beyond the understanding of the people, but he prayed that Sugmad send seekers to him.

He saw Lai Tsi seated outside the cave entrance, the Light of God streaming from his face.

One day a sheepherder passing the cave heard the haunting sound of a lute. He thought the sound came from a demon of the hills. He began to flee. Yet the beautiful strains of the lute's melodies calmed his terror, and he crept near for a look. There, he saw Lai Tsi seated outside the cave entrance, the Light of God streaming from his face. The shepherd recognized the promised Master and drew nearer still. When Lai Tsi touched him in blessing, the shepherd received the bliss of God.

The shepherd rushed home to his family and

neighbors. "The Master with the secret of the true knowledge of God, the Light and Sound, is here among us," he cried.

. Soon, a handful of the chosen few began to gather and became his disciples.

And that's the beautiful story of how Lai Tsi began his mission so many years ago.

Golden Gifts

The kindness of Lai Tsi can be striking. Now let's hear Norma's story about how she learned of it too.

Once, after reading about Lai Tsi before bedtime, Norma asked the Inner Master to lift her up to the inner worlds in the dream state. And she wanted help in remembering her experience, so she could write about it in her dream journal. At 3:30 a.m., she awoke and began a spiritual exercise. Then she fell asleep again and arrived on one of the inner planes in the Far Country.

She began a spiritual exercise. Then she fell asleep and arrived on one of the inner planes in the Far Country.

An old gentlemen approached to offer her a beautiful golden book he'd made for her as a special gift. It would certainly raise her spirits. His face had the kindest and most loving expression she'd ever seen.

Norma awoke in bed and recorded this vivid dream.

Later in the day, she caught a flashback to the prior evening when she'd been reading about Lai Tsi. With a joyful heart, she ran to find a drawing she had of him.

Now she understood. Lai Tsi, with a beautiful

smile, had come to offer her a sacred portion of the Shariyat-Ki-Sugmad. It was the golden book he'd given her in the dream. It was the gift he'd prepared especially for her.

*   *   *

Like Norma, Anita has also met Lai Tsi. She'd been doing the Spiritual Exercises of ECK long before she ever met him in one of her dreams. In her dream, Lai Tsi appeared without dramatic show, except perhaps for a circle of golden cups surrounding him. He spoke via telepathy. He said the cups represented choices of great consequence she'd made at some time in the past.

The next morning, Anita got a nudge to pluck a copy of *The Flute of God* by Paul Twitchell from her bookcase, to read on the bus to work. Later, settled on the bus, she opened the book at random. The page held a passage mentioning Lai Tsi. It said Lai Tsi promised that if people used wisdom to exercise their freedom of choice, they could receive the treasures of heaven. The passage added that infinite possibilities of Spirit can be evoked into forms of power, usefulness, and beauty.

To Anita, the timing and the message were a miracle. She realized it took discipline to make the right choices, even in her thoughts. She saw the golden cups as the forms of power, usefulness, and beauty. Only the Master's love could fill them.

Lai Tsi promised if people used wisdom to exercise their freedom of choice, they could receive the treasures of heaven.

Wayshowers

The ECK Masters seldom try to describe the consciousness of Self- or God-Realization, because it's a highly personal contract with God, between an individual and Sugmad. But the ECK Masters will present the methods, give the spiritual exercises, and show others the way. They are the Wayshowers. They help all who make an honest effort to discover love, peace, and truth. They don't push anyone. All must show the desire and courage to go forward on their own accord.

"Should anyone be in distress or need to reach the great Sugmad," Lai Tsi is quoted in Book Two of *The Shariyat-Ki-Sugmad*, "use this contemplation; repeat it slowly and it certainly brings results." And he gives an ancient seed of contemplation. It will prove of great value to anyone who wants to reach the Source of all creation.

This contemplation will prove of great value to anyone who wants to reach the Source of all creation.

Show me Thy ways, O Sugmad;
Teach me Thy path.
Lead me in Thy truth, and teach me;
On Thee do I wait all day.
Remember, O beloved, Thy guiding light
And Thy loving care.
For it has been ever Thy will,
To lead the least of Thy servants to Thee!

The Window of Heaven

The window of heaven is a skylight all true seekers wish to open.

This window is a bit like a window in Minnesota. After a long, hard winter, it's a welcome relief to open a window and let the spring breeze and birdsongs come gently in. It's a way to say hello to spring. It's also a heartfelt way to say good-bye to the cold, sleet, and snow of winter.

In *The Shariyat-Ki-Sugmad*, Book Two, Lai Tsi further says, "Man seeks too much the gold and silver of the world when he should be seeking the Window of Heaven through which, when opened, all the treasures that he believed were possible will now come pouring to him."

He lists the treasures of Soul. Among them he counts peace, contentment, and happiness. These appear when the Window of Heaven opens.

Lai Tsi adds: "The object of the ECKist, therefore, is peace and wisdom which come from seeking the highest through selflessness."

"Seeking the highest through selflessness." In the simplest terms, it means that the first shall be last, and the last shall be first, a truth that withstands the erosions of time.

Language of Healing

An old Chinese man appeared. He spoke in a soft, beautiful, and yet striking manner.

Years ago, Elena of Norway was shocked at her doctor's order to stay in bed owing to high blood pressure. The diagnosis was very unsettling.

Among her many activities, she loved to share the ECK teachings with others, and this activity would surely suffer. It concerned her greatly.

One night there came a strange dream. She awoke in an unfamiliar setting as an old Chinese man appeared. He spoke in a soft, beautiful, and yet striking and authoritative manner, in a language quite unknown to her. Nevertheless, Elena understood his every word. He revealed what she needed to do to regain her health. And he promised to help.

An instant later, with him at her side, she entered a dense silvery mist. Then came a vague sense of movement, of moving far, far away.

She awoke then. Every detail of her dream remained. Her health condition began to improve soon after. All during her recovery, she wondered about the identity of this diminutive man in her dream.

In time, she made the connection. He was the blessed ECK Master Lai Tsi. She realized that the gift he'd bestowed on her was pure love. It'd come in a most dark and desperate hour.

All during her recovery, she wondered about the identity of this diminutive man in her dream.

The Cave of Unknowing

Sara is an ECK High Initiate who once determined to improve her self-disciplines. She wanted to purify herself spiritually, to be a pure vehicle for the Holy Spirit, the ECK.

One night at bedtime, she did a spiritual exercise. It transported her to a temple in the other worlds, where ECK Masters meet with chelas in their dreams. She'd gone there with a heart full of love, wanting only to serve others. So she became a volunteer. She greeted new arrivals, took them to their appointments, and afterward, escorted them to quiet rooms, where they could contemplate before returning to earth.

After a while, perhaps in recognition of her service to others, Sara received an invitation to choose an ECK Master for a consultation. She chose Lai Tsi.

He asked where she'd like to go. She left it to him, for she was eager to see whatever he wished to show her. Suddenly, the two stood outside the mouth of a cave nestled high in the mountains.

A storm raged. But Lai Tsi paused outside the entrance and told her that when she entered the cave, she'd forget everything: who she was and even where she was. Everything. Yet after she emerged, all she needed from what she learned in the cave would come to mind. She could lie down, symbolically put aside her outer identity, and travel in the other worlds.

This experience with Lai Tsi was in the Cave of Unknowing.

Soon thereafter, Sara noticed a striking change in herself. She now regards the experiences of this lifetime with new respect. The importance of these experiences lies in the spiritual lessons they offer in the quest to become divine love in action.

The importance of these experiences lies in the spiritual lessons they offer in the quest to become divine love in action.

No White or Blue Light, But . . .

Anyone who truly loves God is Its holy instrument. But most people who love God are unconscious of being such an instrument. An ECKist, on the other hand, wants to become ever more conscious of how the Holy Spirit acts through him to uplift others.

So how does this business of being an instrument play out in everyday living? Let's see how it did for Teresa.

Teresa is a Higher Initiate. She once met a businessman who knew little about Eckankar. So she told him of the HU Song, the spiritual exercise that centers our love and attention on one of God's holiest names. She told him how to contemplate.

"And look for a white or blue light," she advised.

She told him of the HU Song, the spiritual exercise that centers our love and attention on one of God's holiest names.

Months later, he called to say he'd be in town on business. He was disappointed to report that the HU exercise hadn't worked: no white light, no blue light. Nothing.

Teresa didn't take his statement at face value, because the ECK prompted her to ask, "So what *do* you see?"

"Nothing but this small Chinese guy with a long white beard!"

She immediately knew it was the ECK Master Lai Tsi. "I'll bring a picture of him when we meet for dinner," she promised.

"Don't bring a picture," he protested. "What if it is him?"

She brought one anyway, and he recognized Lai Tsi at a glance. It's true he didn't see a white or blue light in contemplation, because the Holy Spirit revealed Itself to him through this benevolent and patient instrument of Its boundless love.

Pool of Living Waters

The ECK Masters often give one an experience but let him come to its meaning of his own accord.

One day, Bob did a spiritual exercise in which he stopped by a beautiful pool of water somewhere in the higher worlds. This pool was in a temple, and Lai Tsi had led him to this remote location.

Lai Tsi dipped water from the pool and seemed ready to offer Bob a drink from the dipper. Bob felt privileged and humbled that so great a being as Lai Tsi should do that. But to his great surprise, Lai Tsi poured the water on his head!

And Lai Tsi continued to dip and pour, dip and pour. Bob felt as though a steady stream of water was cascading on his head from far above. The water soon became a torrent. Then, a river.

So Bob took advantage of the situation and swam up the river. And in that way, he entered a higher state of consciousness.

Later, recording the experience in his journal, he realized what Lai Tsi had been trying to show him. It is that Bob lives, breathes, and has his being in the ECK, the Light and Sound of God. He has only to be aware.

Sing HU and imagine Lai Tsi's face before you. There may be a sound of running water or a soft silvery light.

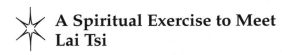 **A Spiritual Exercise to Meet Lai Tsi**

Look at the drawing of Lai Tsi at the beginning of this chapter. Study it a moment or so, and then sing HU. Sing it softly, with eyes shut, and imagine Lai Tsi's face before you on the screen of your mind.

Now pay attention to anything and everything. There may be a sound of running water or a soft silvery light. When Lai Tsi appears, notice his graceful hands or his beautiful, embroidered jacket. Study every detail of his person carefully. Be alert to the light of ECK in his eyes.

In your daily life, practice kindness toward others: to people, animals, and even plants. Ask Lai Tsi to show you ways you may have over-looked. This practice is sure to shower you with the gifts of divine grace.

Kata Daki (*KAH-tah DAH-kee*) is an ECK Master in the Ancient Order of the Vairagi Adepts, who is a woman. Although her true age is beyond belief, she appears to be in her midtwenties to early thirties. Like all ECK Masters, she serves the Sugmad (God) by helping others find the Mahanta, the Living ECK Master.

4
A Woman ECK Master
KATA DAKI

*B*efore we get too far along, we need to say a word about the female members in the Vairagi Order. There are precious few of them in relation to the number of males, and it is for a good reason.

In past ages, and sometimes even today, it was easier for a male to move about in harsh societies and environments. So a Soul that had earned the right to incarnate into a lifetime devoted to the quest for Mastership often chose a male body. It was simply easier to get around in. That is not to say the individual's quest for truth was easier. It was not. Every possible obstacle will appear in such a seeker's life to throw him off the scent of God.

Whether male or female, however, all ECK Masters awaken a deep longing for Sugmad (God) in seekers. Their divine love, care, and attention start many on the road home to God. Indeed, *The Shariyat-Ki-Sugmad*, the holy book of Eckankar, has a word to say about this. In Book Two, it says, "One has only to think of . . . many other ECK Masters, including Kata Daki, . . . to understand the great love, the intensity of which would be a danger to themselves and others if they used it selfishly."

Whether male or female, all ECK Masters awaken a deep longing for Sugmad (God) in seekers.

63

The Beautiful Messenger

Emmanuel, a university student in Ghana, was finishing up some personal work on campus early one July before heading home for summer vacation. The once-bustling campus was nearly deserted.

But as the days went by, Emmanuel found himself in a troubling predicament. His food supply was nearly gone, and he was completely out of money. He had no way to obtain food and no way to get home, so life soon became a day-to-day struggle for survival.

As his hunger worsened, it struck him that he might, in fact, face starvation. So after doing everything possible to help himself, Emmanuel went into contemplation to seek help. He decided to surrender his cares to his inner guide, the Mahanta. And so he fervently sang HU, the ancient love song to God.

To his surprise, a beautiful woman with long honey blond hair appeared on his inner screen.

To his surprise, a beautiful woman with long honey blond hair appeared on his inner screen. She imparted a kind, simple message: "Don't worry, everything is being taken care of."

Could Emmanuel dare to hope?

No sooner had he finished his spiritual exercise than an unexpected knock sounded on the door. It was a friend. He was bearing food: fish, bread, yams, and other vegetables. Emmanuel was both shocked and pleased by the quick response to his desperate cry for a helping hand. A few days later, his father sent money to pay for his trip home.

The first day back with his family, he attended

a HU Chant, a gathering of ECKists who sing the holy name of God. The HU Chant was about to begin. Emmanuel heard someone speak of the ECK Master Kata Daki and how she had helped deliver food to victims of famine. He quickly realized it was Kata Daki who'd come to assure him that all would be well.

Emmanuel felt she'd saved his life. He also expressed a deep love and gratitude for the Mahanta, who'd sent her.

What Is Her Name?

An encounter with Kata Daki brought healing to another man who once faced a life-and-death crisis, but it would be forty years before he'd learn her name.

In 1943, Walter was far from home. Military service had uprooted him to a remote jungle in India, where he suffered an attack of acute appendicitis.

He was informed he'd probably not last the night. The hours passed; the pain increased. Walter knew that if his appendix burst, it would be his last night on earth. So he prepared for the worst.

During the night, in a rare moment of anguished sleep, a visitor appeared to him in a dream—a beautiful, loving woman. She even knew his name.

"It's all right, Walter," she assured him.

And just as she'd said, Walter survived the night, though his appendix did burst. But the deadly toxins drained into his intestines rather

Kata Daki brought healing to another man who once faced a life-and-death crisis.

than into the bloodstream.

Walter made a remarkable recovery. Later, he reflected upon the possible identity of the mysterious dream angel who'd come to offer aid and comfort to him. Had it been his mother? Who else could it be? Yet he remained uncertain. He'd asked his dream messenger her name, and she'd told him, but he couldn't remember it later. It was certainly not that of his mother.

Forty years later, Walter saw a drawing of the very woman of his dream so long ago. "What is her name?" he asked.

Forty years later, Walter discovered Eckankar. Then, one day at an ECK center, he happened to see a drawing of a female ECK Master, a drawing he hadn't seen before. It was the very woman of his dream so long ago.

"What *is* her name?" he asked someone.

When told Kata Daki, he realized this was the long-forgotten name his dream visitor had once given to him. Now, the connection was clear. He finally understood that his dream was a firsthand experience with the divine protection of ECK, through the agency of dear and compassionate Kata Daki.

Who Is Kata Daki?

So we know that Kata Daki is a female ECK Master in the Ancient Order of the Vairagi Adepts, and she inspires in others a longing for God with her benevolence, wisdom, and compassion. Though her true age defies human understanding, she appears to be a young woman of around thirty. She is of average height. Her light brown (honey blond) hair is often shoulder length, but she changes hairstyles to suit her mission.

Like all ECK Masters, Kata Daki serves the Sugmad by helping others find the Mahanta, the Living ECK Master. And like other ECK Masters, Kata Daki takes a special interest in those once close to her in past lives. She guides them to the Wayshower.

She may appear in your dreams wearing a dress, suit, or robe. Whatever fashion she adopts, it fits the time and place. People report a sense of spaciousness and joy while in her presence, for she is a clear channel for the Light and Sound of God.

Kata Daki and all other ECK Masters have an area of special interest to them. Her pet project is to offer assistance to people during great suffering, helping them find food, shelter, and clothing. She is especially active during a war, recession, or famine.

Her face catches one's attention. It reflects a strong character and resolute mind, as do the faces of all the wonderful ECK Masters.

People report a sense of spaciousness and joy while in her presence, for she is a clear channel for the Light and Sound of God.

The Key to Spiritual Freedom

Members of the Vairagi Order, male and female alike, are not into the games that people play—like joining social or political causes. Nor will they hazard their freedom or spiritual potential with a limiting concept such as "the victim of a glass ceiling."

So what is their role? They find joy, satisfaction, and fulfillment by serving as guides so others may find the Mahanta, the Living ECK Master.

For it is he alone who holds the key to spiritual freedom.

An ECK Master's Secret

Jerry determined to resolve a karmic condition that had tormented him for years. An old passion of the mind kept dogging his climb up the mountain of God. Jerry wanted freedom, but how to achieve it with that iron manacle holding him back?

Would the day of spiritual freedom ever come?

About then, Jerry attended an ECK Worship Service. It featured a discussion on the role of the Mahanta, the Living ECK Master and the other ECK Masters who support him by leading Souls to the Light and Sound of God. The topic of the service was "Spiritual Guides Who Show the Way." The officiator presented a spiritual exercise for the audience to try. They were to sing HU, the love song to God. Then they were to focus on meeting a particular ECK Master at the Temple of Golden Wisdom in Chanhassen, Minnesota.

Kata Daki's reply was emphatic. "I gave my heart to God and never took it back!"

So Jerry did the spiritual exercise. In his experience that followed, he noted there were many ECK Masters to choose from when he approached the temple doors. Among them stood Kata Daki. He felt a kinship with her and so followed her out the back doors of the temple, into a garden area.

They walked in silence. Then, inspired, Jerry asked how she'd become so absorbed in God's love.

Her reply was emphatic. "I gave my heart to

God and never took it back!"

Jerry was deeply impressed. These few simple words energized him to realign his goals toward God.

The week progressed, and Jerry's struggle with his old nemesis, the passion of the mind, came to a head. Jerry was forced to face himself. With Kata Daki's words still ringing in his ears, Jerry realized he'd never, ever truly given his heart to God. How could he expect to make headway on the path home to God without such a commitment?

Jerry was forced to face himself.

Jerry then began a spiritual exercise to release his mental burden to the Mahanta, so he could surrender his heart to God.

Jerry is now a freer, lighter, and happier person than ever before. And opening his heart to God has brought more love to his family and others. Finally, he's reached a greater state of being and is now free to go still higher.

A Healing of the Heart

When the ECK blesses someone with the gift of a healing through an ECK Master, it is often in response to some seen or unseen effort first made by the one now in need of assistance.

For example, Carol had a problem with her spine. A surgeon told her a simple surgical procedure would correct it, but the operation went horribly wrong. She spent over five hours in the operating room. There were grave complications later.

As a result, the hospital dismissed the surgeon, and he lost his license to practice medicine.

Carol's anger toward the unqualified surgeon lived on for a long time. One day, though, she read in the obituary page that his wife had died of cancer, and he was left to raise five children alone. Even so, Carol could feel no pity. She felt he deserved his misery for all he'd done to her.

Good Medicine

Years later, health issues from that operation still bothered her. A terrible pain showed up one night in her foot. Opening herself to the ECK, she begged Kata Daki to relieve the agony. Carol was stunned by Kata Daki's response.

"Forgive the doctor," she said.

She told Carol it was necessary to forgive the one responsible for her injury if she ever hoped to be free of the deep bitterness in her heart.

Forgive him? How could she?

Carol finally realized that her emotional attachment would just not release its anger without some kind of help. So she went to bed and called on Kata Daki again. "Kata, help me. Please help me," she pleaded and so fell fast asleep.

In the morning, Carol awoke in much better spirits. Her mind was clear; her heart, happy. She'd found it in herself to forgive the man who'd caused her so much suffering. She even hoped to meet him and his family someday.

So it proved to be Kata Daki's quiet compassion and wisdom the prior evening that had shown Carol how to shed her bitterness.

Carol was stunned by Kata Daki's response. "Forgive the doctor," she said.

Lost and Found

Andrew was shopping at a convenience store. As he stood in the checkout lane ready to pay, a young woman confronted him. "Andrew, baraka bashad!" she said.

Baraka bashad is an ancient blessing well-known to members of Eckankar. It means, "may the blessings be."

Andrew didn't know her, but he returned the blessing. It puzzled him that she'd know him, since he hadn't been to Eckankar activities in years. And she was far too young for them to have met way back then. Andrew asked her to wait for him while he checked out. Her ancient blessing had roused his curiosity.

It only took seconds to pay the cashier, but when Andrew turned to find her, she was nowhere to be seen. He took a quick look around the store, then hurried outside. No woman. He returned to question the cashier. She claimed she'd not seen him speak with a young woman.

Baffled, he drove home.

The incident so haunted him that he decided to contact two ECK friends and tell them of the incident. The ECKists told him of their conviction that his visitor had likely been none other than ECK Master Kata Daki. Andrew had never heard of her.

Kata Daki helps people recover during times of need or tribulation.

One of his friends mentioned how Kata Daki helps people recover during times of need or tribulation. In thinking over his past and how he'd been a bit of a lost maverick of ECK for sometime, Andrew decided that he fit the description of someone who needs help from this ECK Master to get back on track again.

A second happy outcome from his meeting with Kata Daki was this: Besides reigniting his desire for the blessings of ECK, Andrew found that after his encounter with her he'd lost his taste for beer. It was no mean achievement, for he'd indulged in it for well nigh onto fifty years.

Andrew found that after his encounter with her he'd lost his taste for beer.

Kata Daki's mysterious appearance had awakened in him a greater love for God. And so, he had no further need for beer.

Visit from a Friend

Penny was coming down with the flu. But at the moment, she was far too busy to give her health much mind, other than to take some extra herbs and vitamins. There were so many things to do. She had to drive her mate to the dentist for surgery, take care of appointments at work, and prepare for a workshop. Who had time for the flu? Days later, it struck. She finally had to lie down for rest and healing.

Her mate had just left for a trip out of town and had let their two dogs out in the yard before leaving. Penny went to bed and fell asleep.

A Bridge for Love

Suddenly, something jumped up on her bed. Had one of the Great Danes climbed aboard? No, it couldn't be. They were supposed to be outside. Her hands trembling, she peeked over the covers; a cat stared back. Penny sat up for a better look.

It was then that she saw a woman seated at the foot of her bed. The cat darted to the stranger and settled beside her, while the woman stroked its fur. The woman explained that the cat's owners had abandoned it, and that it was now her companion.

Penny and her guest chatted about how some pet owners refused to take responsibility for their pets. The cat, in the meantime, stretched on her back, delighting in the love, petting, and attention from the two women.

They spoke at length. Penny found it easy to pour out her heart, telling of the ways that life had been a challenge to her. Then, after a time, Penny fell asleep. When she awoke, the woman and the cat were gone.

Penny sat up for a better look. It was then that she saw a woman seated at the foot of her bed.

Listening for Love

Penny later came to understand that her visitor had been Kata Daki. The cat's role was to be a bridge of love between them, to ease Penny's fears. Kata Daki had come to offer comfort and care. Startling as this first meeting with an ECK Master was for Penny, she soon came to regard it much like having a friend over. Kata Daki was as real as anyone else. And Penny *had* been wide awake, of that she was certain.

She further understood that she'd received in kind the good she'd earlier done for others. In recent weeks, she'd taken food and given comfort to neighbors who needed a friend.

Her unselfish service had led to this first encounter with an ECK Master. Now when she wants to meet Kata Daki during a spiritual exercise, she first imagines the sweet love that pours from the cat, and then she follows that love to Kata Daki on the inner planes. This connection with Kata Daki helped Penny heal. Able to relax and sleep, she soon recovered from the flu.

Penny also knew she'd witnessed the art of listening, for Kata Daki listened with love and complete attention. And so did her beautiful feline friend.

The ECK Masters are in love with life, and each has the power to arouse a similar love in others for God. All touched by this power will find their hearts opening to the Light and Sound of God.

 A Spiritual Exercise to Meet Kata Daki

Ask Kata Daki to show how to give love to others.

Would you like to learn the secret of love? Note these words from *The Shariyat-Ki-Sugmad*, Book One: "Love does not come to those who seek it, but to those who give love."

Shut your eyes in quiet contemplation. Then sing the word *seva* (see-VAH), a spiritual word that means a service of love. Ask Kata Daki to show how to give love to others. You'll think of ways you've never imagined. She may begin by reminding you of a time you received divine love when you were once in need too.

Kata Daki serves all states of consciousness, from the highest to the lowest. Her wisdom and love are of the highest order, so look for her.

You'll be glad you did.

Shamus-i-Tabriz (*SHAH-muhs-ee-tah-BREEZ*), also Shams-i-Tabrizi (*SHAMS-ee-tah-BREEZ-ee*), is the Adept and guardian of the Shariyat-Ki-Sugmad in the Temple of Sakapori on the Causal Plane. As the Outer and Inner Master of ECK in the thirteenth century, he was the teacher of Jalal ad-Din ar-Rumi, Persian poet, sage, and a follower of ECK.

5
Bard of Ancient Persia
SHAMUS-I-TABRIZ

$\mathcal{L}$isa and her daughters were visiting friends in another state. One night, unable to sleep, Lisa was suddenly aware of a strong scent of jasmine in the dark room. Focusing her attention, she also noticed a separate, distinct aroma of lavender with the jasmine. These two scents brought an expansive and uplifting feeling.

Then, through the light of her Spiritual Eye, she saw two men whom she believed to be ECK Masters.

She recalled a method the Mahanta, the Living ECK Master had once given on how to tell a Master from an impostor: How did one feel after the experience? If uplifted and good, the chela could be assured that his visitor was a real ECK Master. Using this test, she realized that these men were vehicles for ECK.

She recalled a method on how to tell a Master from an impostor.

In the Company of Friends

One of the two Masters turned out to be Shamus-i-Tabriz, from ancient Persia. It was he who said in *The Tiger's Fang* by Paul Twitchell, "No man, no Soul, ever reaches the fulfillment of the quest for God. One goes on and on and on, throughout all eternity, deeper into perfection and deeper into God."

The scent of jasmine is associated with Shamus. He often appears as a thickset man of about forty. His brown beard is short and full. When he is not wearing a turban, one notices his thick, dark brown wavy hair, which looks almost black. His flashing eyes are also a dark brown. On this occasion he was dressed in a robe of gold and red. The turban on his head was golden, a large red jewel in its center, and the color of gold emanated from his being. His presence exuded strength and power.

Shamus appears as a thickset man of forty. His presence exudes strength and power.

But Lisa also sensed a creativity from him, and a keen sense of humor.

A little behind him stood the ECK Master Lai Tsi.

The two Masters showed their presence but spoke not a word. They simply wanted her to know that the love and protection of the ECK were with her.

Prophecy and Protection

A few days after the visit by Shamus and Lai Tsi, Lisa was at a friend's. Near midnight, when it came time to leave, she had a premonition about a car accident. The Inner Master said, "Whatever happens is supposed to happen."

The three-lane highway was slick from a very wet snowfall. Suddenly, the image of the ECK Master Shamus-i-Tabriz flashed in her mind. A second later, without warning, the car spun out of control. She thought of Shamus, relaxed, and felt intense heat rush through her hands to the steering wheel. A force, like a straightedge along the left side of her car, guided the car back into the middle lane. Later, safe at home, she learned that her children had stayed up late to do spiritual exercises at the very time she had narrowly missed having an accident.

Lisa then realized all the help she had received from these channels of ECK: Shamus, and her own children.

Who Is Shamus-i-Tabriz?

Shamus-i-Tabriz, born in AD 1189, was a Sufi master in Persia during the thirteenth century who taught his followers Soul Travel.

While other Sufi masters extolled union with God to their disciples, Shamus, a wandering dervish, led his chosen few to the Light and Sound of God. He was the Outer and Inner Master of ECK in those times, and he gave initiations that lifted chelas, spiritual students, into the conscious state of being.

A prize student was Jalal ad-Din ar-Rumi, a law teacher and theologian. Inspired by his old Master Shamus, Rumi wrote the *Mathnawi*, an epic mystical work of some thirty thousand verses. That poem, by a follower of ECK, defined a pivotal point in the renewal of the Islamic religion. Rumi also founded a group known as the whirling dervishes. They were so named because

Shamus-i-Tabriz was a Sufi master in Persia who taught his followers Soul Travel.

of a spinning dance that induced a trance to release a dancer from his physical body.

Rumi was sufficiently high in consciousness to influence the lives of millions of Muslims and others. The theme of love shows up repeatedly in his writings, for Shamus had revealed to him God's love for Soul.

"Without Love," said Rumi, "the world would be inanimate."

So Shamus helped a once-unconscious theologian and seeker find the waking, trance, and dream states. Rumi's spiritual awakening, in turn, marked a new day for Islam.

"The path of ECK is not a selfish one," reads the second book of *The Shariyat*, "for every time one individual attains perfection, the whole of the human race is lifted up a little higher, just as the yeast leavens the bread."

And how would you recognize Shamus?

He is a broad, heavyset figure of medium height. You'd instantly notice his dark, flashing brown eyes. As said before, his brown beard is short; his dark hair, long. He generally wears a white turban, but sometimes he appears to seekers in a floppy, wide-brimmed hat. So it is hardly unusual, then, to see him wearing a maroon robe flung casually over his left shoulder. His deep, resonant voice is like honey.

Shamus is a true Master of ECK wisdom, a pioneer and explorer of the Far Country. In that regard, he's traced the Sound Current back to Sugmad, the center of all things, and knows It for the essence of the ECK teachings that It is.

The theme of love shows up repeatedly in Rumi's writings, for Shamus had revealed to him God's love for Soul.

Shamus is a truly remarkable man. Count yourself fortunate, indeed, if he chooses to instruct you in the secret knowledge of God.

A Welcome Traveling Companion

Shamus-i-Tabriz turns up at the most unexpected times.

Sherry, a longtime member of Eckankar, lived in a big city and rode the bus to work. She often noticed a certain woman on her bus. This woman appeared to suffer from an illness that caused her to spew uncontrollable profanity. Bursts of verbal abuse would seize her, though as a rule they were directed at no one in particular. Most often, this woman sat alone and discharged her venom at people visible only to herself. Sherry, of course, kept her distance.

On this day, when the woman boarded the bus, Sherry was sitting by a window reading *The Tiger's Fang*, by Paul Twitchell. The seat beside her was vacant. As if drawn by a magnet, the woman sat next to Sherry.

The usual barrage of verbal abuse began as if on cue. Only this time, the woman chose a human target, Sherry, and called her a score of colorful and offensive names. Sherry did not react but kept reading *The Tiger's Fang*. All the while, however, Sherry sang HU to herself.

Sherry did not react but all the while sang HU to herself.

Yet even Sherry's lack of response seemed to anger the disturbed woman who aired opinions on that count too. Sherry paid no heed as the woman made repeated attempts to provoke her, but just sang HU inside herself.

The mad woman stood well over six feet in height and was heavily built. Sherry would have to get past her when the bus reached Sherry's stop. She hoped the woman would not assault her or create a disturbance for the other passengers.

In the next moment, the woman grew quiet. Sherry looked up from her book. Imagine her surprise, yet immense relief, to see Shamus-i-Tabriz alongside the woman. He wore a knee-length purple robe tied with a rope at the waist. A black hat rested casually on his head. Winking, he grinned at Sherry, letting her know that all was in hand. Indeed it was. The ECK Master kept his position of protection until it was time for Sherry to get off at her stop. The woman remained quiet and let Sherry push past her to depart. Shamus grinned again and vanished from sight.

The ECK Master kept his position of protection until Sherry got off at her stop.

As a bonus, Sherry never saw the woman on her bus again.

The Inside Story

The book Sherry had been reading, *The Tiger's Fang,* is the true-life account of Paul Twitchell's journey to the heart of God. In the chapter "Saviors in Limbo," Paul tells of his own encounter with the ECK Master Shamus-i-Tabriz in one of the heavens of God.

"The power of man lies in giving," Shamus had told him. "He must learn to give as Nature, or God, gives."

The Vairagi Masters give people the chance for a freedom they barely know exists. Such opportunities often come as love. One of the greatest blessings of an ECK Master's presence is the discovery of divine love someplace inside you where you would not have thought to look on your own.

The Road to More Love

Lee, a member of ECK from Norway, was looking for just that very thing—divine love. Yet his attitude kept it from him.

One evening Lee awoke in an inner dream experience, walking down a street with a companion. A strange-looking figure came toward them. Lee noticed the man's huge hat, and figuring it was ethnic attire, made a rude comment to his companion about the appearance of the hatted man.

A peculiar thing happened then. As the fellow walked past Lee and his companion, Lee felt a wave of love rush upon him. It was pure love—touching, encircling, and reaching into the inner core of his very being. He could not take his eyes from the man. Lee felt deep love burst from inside him and go to the man walking past them.

At long last Lee could focus on his companion again and, turning, was surprised to see he was of the same ethnic background as the mysterious stranger. He'd missed that particular detail before, and it embarrassed him greatly. Had his companion felt the bite of his slur too? Yet despite the

The Vairagi Masters give people the chance for a freedom they barely know exists.

blunder, Lee felt comfortable being with someone "different" from himself for the first time.

Upon awakening, Lee kept seeing the image of the man in the big-brimmed hat stuck on his head in a happy-go-lucky manner. He soon realized that the stranger was none other than the great ECK Master Shamus-i-Tabriz. In that instant the wonderful feeling of love from Shamus returned once more to surge through Lee's entire being.

This experience with divine love left him a changed and better man.

Seeing with the Spiritual Eye

Everyone seeks more love.

The ECK Masters, like Shamus-i-Tabriz, work with the Mahanta, the Living ECK Master to coax a seeker over the shoals of the human consciousness on the voyage home to God. This help often comes in the dream state.

In ECK our journey begins at the Spiritual Eye. It is the easy way.

In ECK our journey begins at the Spiritual Eye. It is the easy way. A dreamer must ensure that it remains an open window to the higher realms.

Ted was about to learn that simple truth.

Meeting Wah Z, the Dream Master (read more about Wah Z in chapter 11), on the inner planes, Ted would receive an important revelation about the Spiritual Eye. He and Wah Z strolled along the main street of a small town. Wah Z mentioned that none could enter a higher state of unfoldment until every detail of preparation for it was complete. The clarity of this truth confused Ted, perhaps because of its direct application to him.

"This truth may be uncomfortable," said Wah Z, "but it is for your benefit. To understand it, you must surrender to the will of Sugmad."

Ted's mind rebelled against the wisdom of the Mahanta. "Can we talk about this later?" asked Ted. "I need time to think." So they continued on in silence.

"This truth may be uncomfortable," said Wah Z, "but it is for your benefit."

Uncovering the Gift

Soon Wah Z and Ted came to a part of town where Ted's new home was under construction. It was a bright, sunny afternoon, and cheerful workers hurried about their tasks. A ditch lay between the house and the street. However, workers had laid a conduit in the ditch, and one worker was packing and smoothing earth around and over the conduit to create a narrow driveway to the house. Our dreamer later recognized this laborer as the ECK Master Shamus-i-Tabriz.

Ted was impatient to move in. He wanted to add more dirt to the top of the conduit to widen the driveway. That would allow a truck to cross the ditch and deliver new furniture.

Shamus, however, asked Ted to stop adding new dirt. "The earth needs time to settle and dry," he said.

As Wah Z had pointed out, Ted could only move into his new home when all conditions were completely right. So when the furniture truck arrived, the ECK Masters sent it away.

Wah Z called Ted over to Shamus, who knelt by a shiny golden disk on the dirt atop the conduit. With love and care Shamus wiped the dirt from its surface. Tilting the golden disk up for our dreamer to see, he said, "You must never cover this disk with dirt. Keep it clean and uncovered."

Later that day Ted's dream made sense. The new house stood for a new level of consciousness for him on the inner planes. The ECK Masters' ban on a hasty move was a sign that Divine Spirit, instead of self-will, was to manage Ted's life in the future. The golden disk? It was his Spiritual Eye. The dirt suggested delusions caused by material concerns, which can muddy the seeing ability of the Spiritual Eye. But it must remain clear for ECK, the Holy Spirit, to freely shine through it.

This dream gave him compassion for people whose negative habits have trapped them.

Ted now understands the challenge of surrender: Old habits die hard. This dream gave him compassion for people whose negative habits have trapped them. Self-will must drop away. Only then can one enter a higher spiritual state.

Now Ted is all set to move in, so let the furniture truck roll! His new house is completely ready.

Another Chance

In contemplation one day Jeanie found herself alone in a vast wilderness of sand and sky. Far off in the distance was a figure approaching on a horse. As he came into clear view, she recognized him—the ECK Master Shamus-i-Tabriz, an old and dear friend. Yet he rode on by.

Gripped with the feeling of a passing opportunity, she called his name, "Shamus!"

In that instant he was just approaching her again—like a replayed movie scene. But this time he stopped where she stood. Jeanie remembered him from a past life when she'd been a student of ECK and the Mahanta. That was a long time ago. Yet the love bond between them remained unbroken.

"There was something I could not learn from you before," she said. "There was something you were trying to teach me, I could not learn."

Shamus looked at her with his ever-seeing eyes. "You must love God more than your love for God," he replied. He then rode off, leaving her with this enigma.

It took her some time to determine the full import of his cryptic message, even though her heart understood part of it when the words had first left his lips. There was more to love than she knew, than she could see, and more especially to loving God than anything she could imagine.

Through her spiritual senses Jeanie later realized that even beyond what she could know or see today, every part of herself must wholly be given to God in love.

Shamus looked at her with his ever-seeing eyes. "You must love God more than your love for God," he replied.

The Hall of Records

John once received information on a past life from Shamus-i-Tabriz. Shamus took him to the

Sakapori Temple on the Causal Plane.

Chelas (spiritual students) often report that the ECK Adepts are beings of few words. So with no time wasted on greetings, Shamus escorted John down a hallway to the library of records. The long rows of books surprised John. He asked Shamus why these records appeared like books and not like films or videos as others who'd been to the Causal Plane records often described them.

Shamus said, "Little do we realize how our expectations shape our experiences and reality."

They came to a book with records of John's past lives. Shamus showed him which narrative to read.

At length they came to a book with records of some of John's past lives. Shamus showed him which narrative he was to read.

It was about the life of a simple camel driver around the 1300s. John was a Muslim then, making countless trips through the vast expanses of desert. As he journeyed, the silence and emptiness of the desert brought him an intense longing for God.

John also noted a negative trait developing in that life: He began to take on the qualities of his camels. Like them he became less social, loathe to give service to others, even as his camels were unwilling beasts of burden.

John finished his review of that earlier life. Then he asked Shamus what significance it held for him now. Shamus did not give a direct reply. Instead, he offered a clue. He gave an analogy of having a grain of sand in your eye. "Small though it might be," Shamus said, "nonetheless it takes your whole attention and keeps you from seeing until the grain is removed."

John realized he was still learning vital lessons on how to engage in life with his whole being while still practicing the art of detachment.

The ECK Masters can help people see their attachments—numbing layers of insulation that separate them from God's love. The ECK will help all who wish to experience, with no judgments or conditions, the full abundance of God's compassion and love.

Naked in the Love of God

Shamus is a frequent dream visitor, as the next story illustrates.

Annie dreamed she was at a restaurant, standing in line to order food. She had trouble understanding the menu until a kind man came over. His hair was dark, his face clean shaven, and he wore a white robe. He offered a few suggestions. As she was considering them, he said, "Have you been naked in the love of God?"

"What?"

An intense love then began to flow through her, and all sorrow and fear vanished without a trace in this love. She smiled and told him she had in recent dreams.

Food for Soul

Looking into his eyes Annie found herself both swimming and soaring. She began to say, "Your eyes . . ." but he had melted into thin air. By now the food line was backed up behind her. The owner of the restaurant came to offer

The ECK Masters can help people see their attachments— numbing layers of insulation that separate them from God's love.

help, and he assured her that her order would soon be ready.

When her tray arrived, it was so full of food she had to carefully wend her way to a table so as not to spill it.

This dream had much to tell Annie. She knew the man in the robe was the revered ECK Master Shamus-i-Tabriz. Also, the food she received was in fact spiritual food, the Light and Sound of God.

What did it mean to be naked in the love of God?

What did it mean to be naked in the love of God? Annie made a connection to humility—being stripped of attitudes, attachments, and opinions. So being "naked in the love of God" meant to be honest and pure, vulnerable to God's love. The other side to this coin meant not to be attired in the niceties of the social consciousness, a great leveler of spirituality.

Annie's monthly Eckankar discourses dovetailed with her dream experience.

Through them she gained even a deeper understanding of how Soul wears clothes, or coverings, between Itself and God. The ECK Master was helping her see that with more clarity. In order to return to the source of her existence and partake of the ECK, the Audible Sound Current, she must come to know herself as Soul and not as some sort of outer material or covering. All Vairagi Masters have walked the long road of human experience before coming to the supreme enlightenment of God.

So compassion and divine love compel their actions in dealing with people.

A Spiritual Exercise to Meet Shamus-i-Tabriz

Would you like to meet Shamus or another of these agents of the Holy Spirit? Then shut your eyes and begin to softly sing HU.

Imagine that you're in a vast golden desert. The hour is early, and the sun is just beginning to peek over the rippling sands.

Now listen for a sound of tinkling bells off in the distance. Or look for a moving figure on the far horizon. Perhaps the deep, melodious laughter of the ECK Master Shamus-i-Tabriz will ripple out to you in greeting.

Then open your heart to a familiar, ancient friend. You're in good hands.

Such love can begin with small acts of kindness. Let Shamus show you the best ways to start.

The ECK Masters are agents of the Holy Spirit, and their mission is to help you reach the exalted states of God Awareness in this very lifetime, here and now. But such love can first begin with the smallest acts of kindness to those near you.

Go on, let Shamus show you the best ways to start giving love to others.

Rebazar Tarzs (*REE-bah-zahr TAHRZ*) is the Torchbearer of Eckankar in the lower worlds. He was the spiritual teacher of many ECK Masters. Said to be over five hundred years old, Rebazar Tarzs lives in a hut in the Hindu Kush Mountains and appears to many as he helps the current Living ECK Master in the works of Eckankar.

6

Tibetan Adept and Torchbearer of Eckankar

REBAZAR TARZS

It may be that if the ECK Masters developed a close working relationship with followers of ECK in past lives, the students will meet them again in this one. This, despite there being a new Living ECK Master.

One such is ECK Master Rebazar Tarzs. He served as the spiritual leader of ECK years ago, long before the ECK teachings were called Eckankar. A number of his former students have returned to earth in this lifetime, and they often report encounters with their beloved friend and teacher. When asked or if necessary, Rebazar may offer advice on how to clear up a certain difficult situation.

Or it may be another ECK Master, apart from Rebazar, working with selected students from the past, like with a disciple who once gained much in a spiritual way but for some reason then left ECK.

These ECK Masters help today's spiritual leader, the Mahanta, the Living ECK Master. He may call upon them to assist any and all persons. Let's say someone faces imminent danger. Then an ECK Master may come and act as a guardian for him.

Rebazar Tarzs served as the spiritual leader of ECK long before the ECK teachings were called Eckankar.

Who Is Rebazar Tarzs?

Rebazar is a Tibetan who was head of the ECK community many years ago. Tibet was then a spiritual mecca, and the ECK teachings passed by word of mouth, from teacher to pupil.

Rebazar stands about six feet in height and wears a full, neatly trimmed beard as thick as black wool. His hands are large and square, testimony to the rugged outdoor life he enjoys. Meet him during Soul Travel, or otherwise, and you'll see a strong, deeply tanned traveler, master of every possible situation, one whose knowledge of the Far Country is encyclopedic. He has dedicated his entire life to helping others find the perfection of God.

A special feature about Rebazar is his eyes. They're like two dark pools, for they seem to see and know all. Full of compassion and mercy, these all-seeing eyes serve both as a mirror for Soul and a microscope to examine the universe. To look into them is to become lost in the Sound and Light of God, the ECK (Holy Spirit). The liquid of God pours from his eyes. It is like a sweet nectar that offers grace and solace to a burdened heart.

He served as the Mahanta, the Living ECK Master during the superstitious Middle Ages.

Rebazar Tarzs was born in 1461. His childhood home was Sarana, a mountain village in northern Tibet, and he served as the Mahanta, the Living ECK Master during the superstitious Middle Ages. Without the easy access of modern travel, his physical trips were limited. Yet there were followers of ECK all around the world, as there are today. These chelas (spiritual followers) had a strong connection with the ECK teachings by way of the Inner Master, because Rebazar came to them in the Soul body. And thus he could even appear to far-off Native Americans.

But the travels of Rebazar ranged still wider.

He also taught the age-old gospel of ECK to followers in Central America, South America, Australia, China, and what is today Russia. And he met ECKists throughout Europe and Africa. He could accomplish all this because the Mahanta, the Living ECK Master, like all ECK Masters, knows the ins and outs of Soul Travel. It's one of his special talents.

ECK legend, in fact, has it that Rebazar, along with Fubbi Quantz, was involved with the inner guidance of Christopher Columbus.

Rebazar Tarzs is now the Torchbearer of Eckankar. He's still in the same physical body as when he was the Mahanta, the Living ECK Master those many, long ages ago.

As the torchbearer, he steps into the breach between a departed Living ECK Master and that one's successor. Rebazar will then hold the Rod of ECK Power and wear the ECK mantle until the leadership of ECK passes to a successor on the next twenty-second of October.

His direct gaze misses nothing. The robe he wears in the ECK temples is often maroon, but in public he usually appears in clothing more familiar to the locale. He respects this convention of society so as not to excite the curiosity of any who might cause a ripple over a peculiarity, like strange attire.

So how will you know him?

You will recognize Rebazar Tarzs by his dark

Followers of ECK had a connection with the teachings by way of the Inner Master, because Rebazar came to them in the Soul body.

beard, deep brown eyes, and maroon robe, but especially by his direct, no-nonsense manner.

This ECK Master lives in a hut, not due to poverty or a misguided avoidance of comfortable living, for he may appear in lavish surroundings if it suits his purpose. However, he knows that his body—like his humble residence—is simply a place to be in, a shelter to offer refuge from the elements.

The foregoing details offer a good description of Rebazar Tarzs.

He and all ECK Masters are Co-workers with the Living ECK Master and serve Sugmad with a single-minded devotion. The ECK Travelers act as coaches, not mediators, for would anyone dare to come between God and man? They advise people of the most direct route to God.

To illustrate, a football coach can give players the advantage of all he has learned in his own career, yet they, however, must accept their own bumps and bruises on the ball field. After all, isn't the game mainly for them? A good coach would have his team reach the goal line by the quickest, most direct route possible.

A Familiar Gaze

A woman who once benefited from the love and protection of Rebazar is Alma.

Alma, an Austrian, went on vacation to Turkey. Upon arriving at the hotel, she observed a man seated on a low stone wall near the hotel's entrance. His eyes looked familiar, yet she could

You will recognize Rebazar by his dark beard, deep brown eyes, and direct, no-nonsense manner.

not place him. He glanced over, but did not address her.

During her stay, Alma became ill. In despair and exhaustion she called upon the Mahanta for help. The man from the low wall outside the hotel suddenly appeared in front of her bed.

In a loud voice he said, "I am Rebazar Tarzs." His sudden appearance startled her. Uncertain later as to whether she'd been awake or in a hallucinatory fever, Alma nonetheless soon felt better and fully recovered her health.

In a loud voice he said, "I am Rebazar Tarzs." His sudden appearance startled her.

Every day, then, she continued to see the man seated on the stone wall, observing her with those frank, familiar eyes. Who was he?

While at the beach one day, Alma decided to go for a swim. When she made for shore again, a motorboat towing a water-skier drew closer until it was dangerously near. Suddenly, it veered at her; the boaters didn't see her. Fear gripped her, for a collision with the towrope looked certain.

Then the voice of the man from outside the hotel spoke to her, telling her what to do. But no one was there! Alma took the evasive measures the voice had suggested and so saved her life. Others later told her how frightened they had been at seeing her close call. Yet no one mentioned seeing the man who'd given her aid.

Before leaving the hotel for home, Alma was determined to thank the man, but he studiously avoided her. However, when she boarded the bus for the airport, he handed someone a gift for her: an oil painting of a meadow with many tiny flowers. It was not a painting of just any meadow, but a place she'd been to many times in her dream travels. But how could he have known of it unless—

Later, Alma learned the identity of the stranger in Turkey who'd twice come to her rescue when she came upon a picture of the ECK Master Rebazar Tarzs.

Alma's story is one of many that illustrates the love and protection of the ECK Masters, and especially that of Rebazar Tarzs.

ECK Masters You May Have Met

The ECK writings tell countless stories of people like you who've met Rebazar Tarzs or another of the ECK Masters. The role of these Masters is to bring spiritual upliftment to all.

You may have met an ECK Master on the street, and though his identity and role remained unknown at the time, you did sense a lightness and happiness while in his presence. The encounter was a special blessing. And as a result of the encounter, you are sure to learn many secrets of the ages somewhere down the road.

But you must want to.

The Need for Your Permission

One such story is about Tom and Colette from Canada, members of Eckankar, who both saw Rebazar the very same night.

One day Tom shared an idea with Colette. "Since the ECK Masters often come in the Soul

The role of these ECK Masters is to bring spiritual upliftment to all.

body," he said, "and very seldom in the physical body, is it OK with you if we open our home to them?" She agreed. He soon forgot the conversation.

However, their agreement was the permission needed for messengers of Divine Spirit to enter the dwelling of their state of consciousness.

It was because they'd opened their hearts and minds to God.

One night around midnight Tom perched on the cedar chest for his usual contemplative session before sleep. He does the Spiritual Exercises of ECK nightly on account of his deep love for the ECK Masters. Later, as he lay in bed, his thoughts drifted to the Masters. He felt buoyant and happy as he went to sleep.

Happy, spacious thoughts are key if one wishes to succeed with Soul Travel or the dream state.

Quick as thought, it seemed, his eyes opened in the dream state, there to find Rebazar Tarzs. Rebazar enjoys the youthful appearance of a man in perhaps his late thirties or early forties. His black beard is magnificent.

Bemused, Rebazar studied the twenty-five-year-old Tom, who was trying to sprout a handsome beard too. It was all of six weeks old. Nevertheless, the poor thing remained thin and ragged, showing early patches of gray. Rebazar, eyes fixed on it, laughed wholeheartedly. "What a scraggly thing that is," he said.

Thankfully, Rebazar then switched to other matters, until Tom finally fell asleep again.

Happy, spacious thoughts are key if one wishes to succeed with Soul Travel or the dream state.

The Spiritual Law of Returns

When Tom awoke the next morning, he had nearly forgotten his visit from Rebazar until Colette asked, "Did you see anyone in our room last night?"

"No, why?"

"Because a man with a beard was sitting on the dresser."

Tom replied, "That was me. I was doing my contemplation."

"No," she insisted, "you were on the cedar chest. This person was on the dresser, and it was after you went to bed." When she described the mysterious visitor, Tom recalled his dream meeting with Rebazar.

The ECK Master had come to prove that when someone opens his heart to Divine Spirit, the messengers of the ECK will come to bring the blessings of Sugmad (God). It is part of the spiritual Law of Returns.

Invite the ECK Masters to enter the sanctuary of your state of consciousness.

If no dream or Soul Travel meeting occurs the first few times, make further efforts to open your state of consciousness and invite the ECK Masters again. Spend more time experimenting with other spiritual exercises. Others have learned how easy it is to meet the ECK Masters and receive the highest spiritual truths directly, so you can too. Give Tom and Colette's method a try. Invite the ECK Masters to enter the sanctuary of your state of consciousness.

Then watch and wait.

When all spiritual conditions are in order, one

or another ECK Master will appear and bring you blessings from the Most High.

Discourse on the Inner Planes

Robert is a retired minister from California who became a member of Eckankar. Soon after, he began to study *The ECK Dream 1 Discourses* and had an experience with the Mahanta, the Inner Master.

He'd read his ECK discourse at bedtime, shut his eyes, and that was it. The next morning meant rising at four o'clock for work. So he needed rest. But at one-thirty, he awoke and was unable to return to sleep. Finally, however, he did manage to drop off again and awoke in a lifelike dream.

A woman approached him.

"I'm Harold Klemp's wife," she said. "I want to welcome you to Eckankar. My husband will help you anytime and in any way he can." Then Wah Z (a name for me on the inner planes), the Inner Master, entered the room.

His wife continued, "I want to introduce you to my husband."

Wah Z repeated, "Yes, I will help you in any way I can."

Robert was left with the very strong impression that this meant: "I will help you only if you want the help. I will not intrude in your space in any way, because to do so would be to risk my own freedom."

Someone far along the spiritual path will never try to lure another to his own path or belief. A Spiritual Traveler knows that doing such a thing to another fastens the chains of bondage to his

When all spiritual conditions are in order, one or another ECK Master will appear and bring you blessings from the Most High.

own arms and legs. Where would his spiritual freedom be then?

Wah Z now said, "I'm going to whisper your secret word to you." Robert awoke with a start, his spiritual mantra fixed indelibly in his mind.

This secret word is a personal key that the Mahanta imparts to every initiate of Eckankar, to open him to a deeper and more intimate relationship with the Holy Spirit. This word tailors one's state of consciousness to the Holy ECK.

Sleep was slow to come after Robert's momentous dream, and he grew worried. Four o'clock was coming fast. He needed sleep desperately. He shut his eyes and tried to sleep again.

Suddenly, Rebazar Tarzs stood before him. This, too, occurred on the inner planes, but the experience was more real than ever. Rebazar and Robert greeted each other like old friends. They hugged. Then Rebazar said, "I've been working with you and your wife."

He was sure he hadn't been asleep. He'd been wide awake. Rebazar was actually with him in the Soul body!

Robert couldn't believe it—he'd met two ECK Masters in a single night. "This sort of stuff happens to other people, not to me," he said.

Rebazar Tarzs stayed for two hours, until four o'clock arrived. Robert dutifully rolled from bed to clean up for work. And oddly enough, he felt no unusual tiredness the whole day.

Over the next two weeks Robert pondered his dramatic reunion with Rebazar Tarzs. He was sure he hadn't been asleep. He'd been wide awake. Rebazar was actually with him in the Soul body! Robert sorted through a pile of doubts, and an undeniable fact came to light. *It's true. It's true,* he thought, *what the ECK Masters and what the Mahanta, the Living ECK Master have said, it's true.*

Yes, you can count on them to appear when the appointed time has come, even if it happens to be in the middle of the night.

The Mahanta, the Living ECK Master and all ECK Masters meet all who love truth and the Holy Spirit, and wish to learn the wondrous ways of enlightenment they're entitled to.

An Excited Aussie

I once received a letter from Jack, an Australian, who'd written several times before. He'd been hunting for a teaching position and had finally landed a choice assignment in Kuwait. His journey there was to begin soon, and he hoped to start teaching in the fall. But while awaiting confirmation of his assignment and more about what the future might hold for him, Jack decided to help out at a local ECK center in Australia. He had the pleasure of some fascinating conversations with people who'd dropped in to discuss ECK principles.

One day another Aussie raced up the steps and into the ECK center, shouting at the top of his lungs, "I can't believe it! I can't believe it!"

As the fellow burst into the room, Jack asked, "What can't you believe?"

"Two days ago I had a dream," the other said. "This man with a beard came and with him was this shining blue light." (Eckankar is all about the Light and Sound of God, of course.)

"Two days ago I had a dream," the other said. "This man with a beard came and with him was this shining blue light."

The speaker was the picture of wonder and excitement. He exclaimed, "This man was very striking!" And staring at a wall, he said, "His picture is one of these portraits hanging on the wall."

Jack asked, "Which one of them did you see in your dream?" The man pointed to Rebazar Tarzs.

Rebazar had thus appeared to the seeker, accompanied by the Blue Light of the Mahanta. This color, in particular, has a deep significance in the ECK teachings.

Why Me?

The ECK Masters often come in people's dream states, while at other times they offer direct aid physically when someone in trouble needs help.

The ECK Masters mingle with people still today. Oftentimes they come in people's dream states, while at other times they offer direct aid physically when someone is in trouble and needs immediate help.

These little-known Masters surely do exist. Their sole mission is to encourage and help Souls who want to return home to God.

When the time is right, an ECK Master will make his presence known to you. It may be someone like Rebazar Tarzs, or Peddar Zaskq (who, as Paul Twitchell, founded the modern-day movement of Eckankar). So when a seeker is ready, an ECK Master appears and lends a hand. Yet he often comes in disguise.

You may ask, Why would they help me, a stranger? After all, I'm Christian. I don't believe in ECK Masters.

But remember a basic doctrine of ECK is reincarnation. Most all who come to Eckankar today were followers of ECK long ago and disciples of one of these ECK Masters.

Their pictures are readily available for this reason. The pictures are in ECK books and on posters at ECK centers. This aid is for new and old in ECK alike. Newcomers may thus have a chance to recognize one of their dream teachers, these wonderful Adepts in the Ancient Order of the Vairagi.

So the ECK Masters act as people's advisers and guardians, and may remain with these chosen few for an entire lifetime. And sometimes, indeed, they've appeared years before these people even heard of Eckankar.

How Michael Became a Seeker

Michael, a young African of twenty-two, is another example of someone meeting an ECK Master years before finally coming into Eckankar.

He'd suffered all kinds of financial setbacks. In addition, he also grappled with a serious health problem: his eyesight was failing. His relatives thought him a handsome and a clever young man, albeit poor. His father was ill, and the family was poor like Michael. He'd developed a deep concern. He did not wish to be a burden on others, so he offered up a prayer to God.

He repeated this prayer nightly. Then one night he was lifted from his body.

He pleaded, "God, please take me from this vale of tears. I have had as much as I can take of this physical world." He repeated this prayer nightly.

Then one night he was lifted from his body, perhaps in a similar way as Paul, the apostle, who said he had known a man caught up even unto the third heaven. Michael's own Soul Travel experience began like this: He'd fallen asleep on his bed and in the next moment awakened in a whole different world. It was such a beautiful realm! The temperature felt just right, and an enormous amount of light illuminated the entire landscape. Everything shone with a refreshing goodness, alive with love and compassion.

"I like this place," he decided. "I'd like to stay."

Two men stepped from a nearby hut. One wore a thick black beard and would do all the talking for both of them. Much later, long after this experience, Michael would come to recognize him as the great ECK Master Rebazar Tarzs. But for the moment he had no inkling of this man's identity or even of the location of this enchanted land.

The black-bearded one said, "Why are you here?"

Michael replied, "I'm here because I'm sick of earth and this is a nice place. I think I'd like to stay here with you." He explained his prayer to God and added, "I've been praying to God to get me away from earth, and it looks as if it's worked. I think I'd like to stay."

Michael looked around at the sparkling blue sky. Then he noticed a light shining from the little hut, a blue light. It appeared to originate from no identifiable source. It rather seemed to flow from everywhere at once. Quite unknown to him, it was the Light of God, often seen as the Blue Light of the Mahanta.

Now the black-bearded one said, "You can't

A blue light seemed to flow from everywhere at once. It was the Light of God, often seen as the Blue Light of the Mahanta.

stay. You have to go back."

Michael balked. "No, I won't go back. I shall stay." He repeated all the reasons for his unquenchable desire to remain in this heavenly world of love and beauty.

However, the other said, "It's impossible. You haven't finished your mission on earth."

"That may be, but I'm not going back."

Rebazar Tarzs came over and kindly took his hand. The next thing Michael knew he was in his room again and awakening. He sat up in bed and exclaimed, "What was that?"

Going to Heaven

It's a curious thing about people who enjoy an easy life, a good living with everything handed to them without effort, sweat, or trouble. They often have no longing for God or truth.

The blue light, which Michael reported, issues from the Mental Plane, St. Paul's third heaven. The Spiritual Travelers of ECK know of different levels in heaven. However, St. Paul's statement about that fact is the lone biblical reference to it. This mention, of course, presupposed heavens one and two. Who was to say there weren't four, five, or more?

Michael was puzzled by his out-of-body experience, so he approached the parish priest with a swarm of questions like, What did his Soul-shaking experience mean? Where was this splendid land of warmth and beauty?

While in that higher world, Rebazar Tarzs had

Michael was puzzled by his out-of-body experience, so he approached the parish priest with a swarm of questions.

asked him, "Do you know where you are?"

The question suggested that the place did have a name to identify it. His curiosity wished for an answer. The priest would surely know.

But the priest had no idea where the place was or even what Michael's experience meant. Yet Michael gained hope from it, and he no longer asked God to remove him from this world. Whatever his purpose might be here, Michael realized it was not finished.

And so, he joined a company that for ages before him had engaged in the self-same pursuit of God. In time he would find ECK books and begin to satisfy that eternal longing.

Much later Michael would recognize Rebazar Tarzs as the very man who'd met him outside the little hut in those upper reaches of heaven.

In one such ECK book he would much later find a picture of Rebazar Tarzs. And Michael would recognize him as the very man who'd met him outside the little hut in those upper reaches of heaven.

It was then that Michael would begin to satisfy his long-standing desire to learn who and what he was.

ECK Masters Really Do Exist

Another newcomer also received help and insight from Rebazar before becoming a member of Eckankar. So let's look at a guiding experience Phil once had in his quest for truth.

Phil was still a student when he happened upon the ECK teachings on a university campus. They so intrigued him that he obtained the classic book *ECKANKAR—The Key to Secret Worlds* and tried the Spiritual Exercises of ECK in it.

The Christmas holidays began a few weeks later, so he went home to spend them with his family. He awakened one morning to the sound of his parents' voices, but since it was too early to rise, he rolled over and tried to get some more sleep.

Phil still lay awake, but with eyes shut, when he spotted a pinpoint of distant light on the inner screen of his mind. And then he was suddenly sweeping upward toward the light at an incredibly fast speed. A moment later he gazed down at the beautiful earth from a vantage point high in space. It was the first time he had been out of the body.

The experience, as you may well imagine, mystified him completely.

Then in a dream about a year later, Phil was having a terrible time in the other worlds. He tried to scream and so awaken from sleep. When he did finally manage to open his eyes, he was startled by the figure of a dark, hooded shape leaning over his bed.

Now what? he wondered. If it wasn't one thing, it was another.

Phil took a good look at the figure and observed a bearded man with soft, calm eyes. All fear left Phil in a heartbeat. (At a much later date he would see a picture in an ECK book and thus identify the mystery man as Rebazar Tarzs.)

The ECK Master had begun to speak. However, Phil couldn't make out any of the words. It was as if Rebazar were speaking in a tunnel, from some other dimension. Phil realized with a start that he could look right through the ECK Master,

Phil took a good look at the bearded man with soft, calm eyes. All fear left in a heartbeat.

who'd come in some sort of light body. But why was he here? It was simply to relieve him of his frightful dream, and also to assure him there really were friendly beings like the ECK Masters.

Phil's nerves had settled down by the time he swung his legs from bed.

In the day's mail was his first ECK discourse. Then Phil understood that Rebazar Tarzs had come to tell him: You've made a commitment to ECK, and now the secret teachings begin.

He also understood something else. The fact that he could see Rebazar as clearly as any human being but remain unable to hear his words meant that the real teachings come in a special way, to ensure that only the worthy can receive them. They come via the secret inner channels of communication.

And that's how Phil's spiritual education began.

Rebazar Tarzs had come to tell him: You've made a commitment to ECK, and now the secret teachings begin.

Teresa Overcomes Low Self-Esteem

Teresa once wrote to me of a special experience she'd had with Rebazar on the inner planes. He helped her overcome a problem of low self-esteem.

During this inner sojourn she met him at a mountainside hut. They both wore the rough clothing of berry pickers, with a heavy shawl-type material over their heads and necks to afford protection from the blazing sun. She followed closely on his heels along a steep mountain path. At one point the path dipped into brush, and they emerged at a completely different spot on the trail, about two miles down the road, on the outskirts of a rustic village. The shortcut was such that it felt like no more than a single giant step. It was one of Rebazar's shortcuts. His hut, more like a way station, had many secret trails leading to and from it.

Rebazar's hut, more like a way station, had many secret trails leading to and from it.

The figure of a man came into view a few yards down the road. Gnarled, old, poor, bent, and alone, he was only scratching out a bare living.

With sudden animation Rebazar's voice boomed, "I'll never get a good enough price for these berries in the market! Man, come eat some if you want!"

The old man approached, expecting a handout of picked-over berries. But when the lid came off Rebazar's basket, it was full of lush, beautiful, glistening fat berries—purple and fragrant jewels. They were the most perfect berries one could imagine.

Teresa watched the old man closely. She wondered, *Do special berries go to special people? Could an ordinary man partake of the extraordinary? What about the Law of Economy? Would the old man feel greedy, poorer, or too unworthy—and dismiss the gift of these choice berries as one-time luck?*

This encounter awakened her own feelings of low self-esteem.

Then her observations took a turn. She felt the presence of the Mahanta in her heart. He said, "Or does he put all that aside and eat them wisely, appreciating and acknowledging their fine, fine, quality and not judge himself through the eyes of berries?"

Ouch, his observation surely did hit home.

Teresa realized she had the problem of judging herself as if through the eyes of berries, or anything else, because of her unwillingness to use her own eyes. She was fixed on faults instead of virtues. Well, she did have eyes, but she wasn't using them in the right way. How seldom she bothered to look through the eyes of her true self. But she now knew that the Mahanta's unwavering patience would take chelas (spiritual students) further than their own limitations. At last she could accept the gift of love and self-esteem that Rebazar held out to her.

If the old man, too, had had the grace and dignity to accept spiritual gifts from the Master into his life without tearing them to pieces with his mind, measuring them against his little self, he indeed would have discovered how rich and elegant a spiritual being he truly was.

Rebazar certainly had gained Teresa's full love and respect.

A stranger, whose entire body radiated with light and love, woke Ben and said to follow him.

An Encounter with ECK Masters

In December 1997, Ben, an African, was seriously injured by bandits. He was being taken to Abidjan, Côte d'Ivoire, for emergency medical care. It was then that Ben had the following dream.

A stranger, whose entire body radiated with light and love, woke Ben and said to follow him. Such was the trust he inspired that Ben did so without a moment's hesitation. Soon they came to a door. The stranger opened it, revealing a large, brightly lit courtyard. In it stood a small hut whose door was nothing but a woven mat. Lifting the mat, Ben came into the presence of his grandfather, who'd died several years before.

"What do you come to find here?" his grandfather asked.

The old man went on. He explained that he himself was waiting for Ben's mother, who'd died in December 1996. She had to complete a final task before moving on to a permanent home in a higher plane. Then he called, "Veronique." A voice replied, "Papa," and she appeared.

Lifting the mat, Ben came into the presence of his grandfather, who'd died several years before.

The old man asked her to accompany Ben to the hospital and further instructed her which doctor should care for him. But she must not let "Doctor X" give him the least bit of care. On the other hand, the services of "Doctor Y" could be allowed without any reservation.

"So take the stool," he instructed her, "and sit in the hospital at my grandson's side to pick out the doctor who must care for him!"

Indeed, Doctor X was the very first doctor to come, but Veronica opposed his help vigorously. At the appearance of Doctor X, Ben became highly agitated. His battle with Doctor X in his sleep was so violent that Ben fell off the bed.

Another patient in the room sent an urgent call for the nurses' help. They awakened Ben. That put an end to his dream.

After Ben had returned home, his wife understood the significance of his dream and suggested he look for an ECK center. He should become a member of Eckankar. Her advice was right to the point.

The name was foreign to him. Ben did not know that Eckankar was a spiritual teaching, nor how his wife had learned of it. By chance he ran into a friend who turned out to be an ECKist. The friend introduced him to the HU Song and other ECK activities. Thus it came about that while visiting the ECK center Ben recognized the portrait of Rebazar Tarzs. He was the stranger in his dream who'd led him to his grandfather.

This experience was Ben's confirmation that Eckankar is truly a universal teaching. It speaks to all.

This experience was Ben's confirmation that Eckankar is truly a universal teaching. It speaks to all, not only to ECKists.

So Ben and his family are now members of Eckankar. They are grateful for the blessings of ECK and the assistance of ECK Masters like Rebazar Tarzs.

Reality of the ECK Masters

The ECK Masters of the Order of the Vairagi Adepts help the Mahanta, the Living ECK Master spiritually uplift all people. They routinely appear to fortunate Souls years before these people ever step onto the path of ECK. The ECK Masters prepare the way.

Many other ECK members also recall meeting Rebazar Tarzs before they became ECKists. Ellen is one such initiate. She recounts an experience in which she did the Spiritual Exercises of ECK. Suddenly she was on a grassy knoll talking with the legendary Rebazar Tarzs. He was dressed in a knee-length maroon robe and carried the large staff that he commonly uses while roaming the mountain wilds.

He discussed several topics with her.

Abruptly, then, he sprang up and broke his large, strong oak staff over his knee as easily as if it were a piece of kindling. Ellen felt uneasy. Had she upset him? What spiritual lesson had she failed to understand?

With a start, Ellen then understood. Rebazar had removed some of her karma when he broke his staff. She'd mastered all the lessons connected with that particular karma, so he'd taken it from her.

This experience taught Ellen to recognize the love and help that the ECK Masters do give. Their assistance reaches well beyond the physical plane, which, after all, reflects only a small portion of the total spiritual unfoldment of anyone.

Unfoldment, then, as does the ECK Masters' aid, reaches far into the inner worlds. Much ancient karma awaits a final resolution there.

See Things for What They Are

Everyone is special to God. For that very reason, everyone is also special to the ECK Masters. So no problem is too trivial for them.

Paula was having a problem with one of the five mind passions of lust, anger, greed, vanity, and an undue attachment to things. And she was about to repeat an old mistake. She was all set to make rash promises to God like, "I'll never do this again."

She'd begun beating herself up for backsliding when Rebazar Tarzs's voice cut sharply into her thoughts.

Everyone is special to God. For that very reason, everyone is also special to the ECK Masters.

"Stop doing this!" he ordered.

Her longtime friend appeared in her inner vision. In his hands he held an old, well-traveled pair of shoes from her closet. She pointed out their scuff marks.

Rebazar said, "The human consciousness is much like these shoes."

He made clear that the purpose of new shoes wasn't just to keep them in brand-new condition, but to walk in them. So it was natural for them to be scuffed.

"The purpose of the human conscious-ness," he explained, "is to get you from here to God, to walk from here on your journey home."

"The purpose of the human consciousness," he explained, "is to get you from here to God, to walk from here on your journey home. And if you live life fully, it will look a little like these shoes. It will be a little worn; there will be a few scuff marks.

"You are putting too much of your God energies into working over this problem. It is not that big a deal. If you really don't like it, polish your shoes."

It was a relief for Paula to hear that.

Before Rebazar left, however, he added, "We see things for what they are."

Paula understood the implied meaning. The ECK Masters see things for what they are—and love them dearly, because each life is God's personal handiwork. The ECK Masters work like a tuning fork to one's human consciousness, to one's attitudes and thoughts.

The relationship between Soul and God is of paramount interest to the Mahanta, the Living ECK Master, as well as to all the ECK Masters.

Rebazar's appearance was a great comfort to Paula. It cast a whole new light on things. If something she did was holding her back spiritually, then she must do something better. She must polish her shoes. There was certainly no room for guilt in a healthy state of consciousness.

What a valuable lesson to learn.

 A Spiritual Exercise to Meet Rebazar Tarzs

Relax in contemplation with eyes shut. Picture yourself on a beach, walking in sand at the ocean's edge. The warm waters dance about your feet, and a light ocean spray splashes a refreshing coolness on your face. Overhead, silent white gulls sail upon the wind.

Now breathe in as the waves gently wash toward you. Then, on the outgoing breath, sing *Rebazar* (REE-bah-zahr) softly in rhythm with the waves fleeing back to the sea. Do this exercise twenty to thirty minutes a day. After you're skilled at it, Rebazar or another ECK Master will come and impart the wisdom of God to you.

Do this exercise twenty minutes a day. Rebazar or another ECK Master will come and impart the wisdom of God to you.

At first you may feel you have met Rebazar or one of the ECK Masters only in your imagination. But with time and practice, you will find they are real people just like you.

Towart Managi (*TOH-wahrt mah-NAH-gee*) is the ECK Master in charge of the Shariyat-Ki-Sugmad in the Temple of Golden Wisdom in the city of Mer Kailash on the Mental Plane. As guardian, his title is the Koji Chanda. He was the Mahanta, the Living ECK Master in Abyssinia, an ancient kingdom in what is now Ethiopia.

7
African Holy Man
TOWART MANAGI

The ECK Spiritual Guides can seem to simply appear out of the mists of time to help any Soul seeking love, truth, and the awareness of God. They come by day, by night, at times of great trouble or need, or in disguise to bring comfort to an old friend—perhaps someone like you.

Who Is Towart Managi?

There are many ECK Masters of every race. The foremost black ECK Master known in the ECK writings is Towart Managi. He was the Mahanta, the Living ECK Master in Abyssinia, an ancient kingdom in what is now Ethiopia. Today, he is the ECK Master in charge of the Shariyat-Ki-Sugmad on the Mental Plane.

The Temple of Golden Wisdom there is the Namayatan Temple in the city of Mer Kailash. The temple is similar in appearance to the temple of Diana in Ephesus, where Eckankar was taught in ancient times.

Towart Managi was an African holy man during his spiritual leadership in Abyssinia. Slight of stature, he appears more or less delicate, with

There are many ECK Masters of every race. The foremost black ECK Master known in the ECK writings is Towart Managi.

closely cropped hair and a small white beard.

The Real Path to God?

When a doubtful seeker wondered, *Which is the right path for me?* Towart Managi helped her receive an answer.

Bobbie had many experiences with ECK Masters as a child. She often dreamed of the love of God as Light and Sound, but in growing up, she lost sight of her search for God as the number-one priority in her life. At the end of high school, however, she came across a teaching from India that had a certain appeal for her.

Was it her path to God?

Three years later, she found *The Tiger's Fang* by Paul Twitchell. Bobbie discovered in reading it that Paul described some of the very places she'd traveled to on the inner planes—only Paul had gone far beyond her experiences. He had been to the very heart of God. This new information seemed only to bring confusion to her situation. Which was her real path to God? How would she know, and could she have a sign?

Then Bobbie had a dream that left no doubt as to which spiritual path was the best one for her.

In the dream, ECK Master Towart Managi was holding a conversation with the leader of the Indian path she'd encountered in high school. She listened with great care to the points made on either side of the discussion. In the end, the path that lit up for her was that of Eckankar. It was a sure sign. Still in a later conversation with Towart, she'd ask, "Why do I need to follow any outer path? Why can't I just receive everything now, in this moment?"

Towart threw back his head and laughed with unconcealed merriment. He asked if she were to build a boat, would she gather up her best estimation of building materials and then start experimenting, starting over time and again, to reinvent a boat? Or would she be willing to go to boatbuilding school and graduate?

A most persuasive point.

So upon awakening in the morning, Bobbie sent for her Eckankar membership. She'd found her answer and especially the true Satsang (study of the ECK works) she'd been seeking since childhood. In that life-changing dream, Towart Managi had helped her find answers to her search for the Master, the Sound Current, and the true initiation.

Her meeting with the ECK Master thus removed all doubt about which path was the right one for her.

A Spiritual Experiment

David learned that Eckankar was soon to publish a portrait of the ECK Master Towart Managi. He took this as a unique opportunity to test his inner experiences with the Spiritual Exercises of ECK. David would try to meet this Master on the inner planes before the picture's release and see how the two images matched up.

So he asked the Mahanta for a meeting with

She'd ask, "Why do I need to follow any outer path? Why can't I just receive everything now, in this moment?"

Towart. Nothing seemed to happen, however. About a week later, David awoke in a dream where he was traveling with a group of people to see the famed ECK Master Towart Managi in person.

Great Waves of Love

At the meeting, David observed how Towart Managi was not waving his arms about, drawing attention to himself. He was relaxed and casual. And yet the moment David's eyes met Towart's, he felt an unexpected rush of tears. The divine love flowing from this humble being was nearly too great to bear. It went straight to his heart. He looked away for a moment and saw a Hispanic man beside him, and his eyes were wet with tears too.

In spite of the ECK Master's diminutive body, the presence of God flowed strongly from him in gigantic waves.

David noted Towart's slender stature. In spite of the ECK Master's diminutive body, the presence of God flowed strongly from him in gigantic waves. Many times, David's gaze returned to Towart. There he found a love beyond all human understanding.

Later, comparing the Towart Managi of his inner experience with that of the portrait, David was satisfied that the artist's rendition was a true likeness of this ancient ECK Master.

Preparing to Meet a Spiritual Traveler

In the Dominican Republic, Ava attended an ECK introductory event titled "How to Become the Spiritual Adventurer." She was a newcomer to

Eckankar. The focus of the event was to show people how to make a connection with one of the ECK Masters—Spiritual Travelers—to serve as their guide on a spiritual adventure in faraway places beyond human imagination. A spiritual exercise was given at the event. Ava tried it. Soon she met Towart Managi during contemplation and chose him to be her spiritual guide and counselor.

The next week, in a follow-up class, she told her story.

Ava worked in the natural-healing field. She'd once tried a cleansing regimen on herself but had become terribly sick from the detoxification's side effects. Ava tried every method she knew to counter the healing crisis. But nothing offered relief.

Focusing on Towart Managi had produced an instant, quantum leap in healing.

Making the Connection

Then she remembered the earlier connection she'd made in a spiritual exercise with Towart Managi and, in desperation, asked his help. She told the class that focusing on him had produced an instant, quantum leap in healing.

Yes, the Spiritual Exercises of ECK did work. And at least one of the ECK Masters was real. She could attest to that.

In class the following week, Ava told of a second connection. She and a friend had gone for a swim in the ocean. Her friend had attended the ECK event too. The Atlantic was a bit unruly that day, but the two women were unaware that the waters hid a treacherous undertow. The current carried them far from the deserted shore. Ava was losing the struggle with the current. She realized that nothing she could do anymore would bring her safely to land again. Her friend grappled with the same bleak fate.

Thoughts of drowning crowded in. Then Ava remembered to lock her attention on Towart Managi. She called to him in despair. The next moment, a huge wave rose behind Ava and her friend and bore them safely to shore.

Ava emphasized to the class how the miraculous appearance of that one gigantic wave was nothing short of divine intervention. She had no doubt about the lifesaving help she'd received through her connection with Towart Managi.

A Respectful Answer

Nick, an Australian, planned an ECK workshop in his area. His idea was to unite the ECK community in its common mission of presenting the ECK teachings to the public. In preparing for this leadership meeting, Nick wished to highlight things that would inspire harmony. It would cut down on personality tussles among some leaders. So he set out to develop a handful of spiritual exercises, to gain a better understanding of how to ensure accord and goodwill among the leaders who'd be in attendance.

One idea Nick had was this: to meet an ECK Master inwardly with whom he was currently working and seek his counsel. So Nick chose the Abyssinian ECK Master Towart Managi. Soon after, Nick met him in contemplation.

She called to him in despair. The next moment, a huge wave rose behind Ava and her friend and bore them safely to shore.

"What do the ECKists here need to do to let this area grow?" he asked.

Towart said, "Respect is needed."

"Respect?"

The word held negative connotations for Nick. He felt it was what elders or people in power demanded of others.

But Towart continued where he'd left off.

"Respect one another. You are each of the body of the Mahanta. Everyone is of the body of the Mahanta and deserves the utmost respect. This brings out the higher qualities of Soul in those we are around."

Nick thus learned about the element of surrender in this new insight on respect. He further realized that to see the Mahanta in others calls for a surrender of oneself to a higher power. That power is ultimately vested in the ECK (Holy Spirit).

Towart said, "Respect one another. This brings out the higher qualities of Soul in those we are around."

The Healing Garden

Samuel, a doctor in Nigeria, has had many experiences showing him the spiritual gold available in the Spiritual Exercises of ECK. Ill himself once, he had looked to the Mahanta to relieve the fear of his troubling disease. The Mahanta had lifted him to a garden on the Astral Plane. There, the Mahanta directed him to another ECK Master. This Master never did reveal his face. He did, however, tell Samuel to eat certain leaves in the garden. The doctor did so.

This experience on the inner planes led him to make further experiments with herbs to control his disease. He thus created a mixture that was to be taken as a drink twice a day. The formula of garden herbs allowed him to cut back significantly on the synthetic drugs he'd taken up till then.

The herbal mixture was very successful. He soon began to prescribe it for his own patients, with highly satisfying results.

Golden Tools of ECK

One night, Samuel dreamed of traveling a lonely road. Beautiful bushes, shrubs, and trees of many colors lined the road, and the air in that world was fresh and clean. After a time, a young boy appeared. He informed Samuel that the road had taken him into a local government area of Ethiopia.

The scene shifted. The doctor found himself in a new place with different people. A youngish man there inspired such confidence in Samuel that soon the two of them headed into the brush in an unaccountable search for gold. People were digging on every side. As the doctor's spade turned the soil, he saw that the entire area and even his tools were of a golden hue. Every item he unearthed was golden too. His spade turned up a golden knife, golden pots, and even a golden sword, so he kept digging, hoping to find more golden treasures.

Yet an odd phenomenon was that not any of the other people were finding such riches.

"Why?" he asked the man beside him, who

As the doctor's spade turned the soil, he saw that the entire area and even his tools were of a golden hue.

seemed well acquainted with this area and its people.

His companion replied, "It is not yet their time to dig out gold."

When Samuel awoke, he remembered chanting the name of ECK Master Towart Managi during his spiritual exercises before bedtime. He realized that the little boy's role in the dream had been to tell of the connection between his dream and Ethiopia, the area of Africa where Towart had once served as the Mahanta, the Living ECK Master.

The youthful companion who'd inspired such a feeling of confidence in Samuel was none other than Towart Managi. Although the doctor's dream had opened on the Etheric Plane, the change of scene to the area where everything was golden indicated that Towart had taken him higher still, into the first of the true heavenly worlds, the Soul Plane.

What a blessing!

There, Samuel learned, everything in the high heaven of the Soul Plane is of the purest and finest spiritual gold that anyone could ever hope for. His discovery was a direct result of a Spiritual Exercise of ECK.

The doctor's dream had opened on the Etheric Plane. Towart had taken him higher still, into the first of the true heavenly worlds, the Soul Plane.

Golden Words of Love

Yvonne from New Zealand flew home from an ECK Worldwide Seminar, a portrait of Towart Managi stowed safely in her bags. Once home, she studied the portrait with great care. She felt he was really an old, close friend. She asked the Mahanta in contemplation to introduce her to Towart.

Yvonne soon after awoke on the Mental Plane, in the company of Towart Managi, guardian of the Shariyat-Ki-Sugmad (the ECK bible) in the exotic city of Mer Kailash. He escorted her to the place where that section of the Shariyat is on display. Yvonne immediately recognized it by white light glowing around it. Words streamed into her mind in the form of this poem:

> *It is about love,*
>
> *always love.*
>
> *Do everything*
>
> *with love.*
>
> *Do what you love to do.*

(silence)

> *You were there*
>
> *when we created*
>
> *the stars, the worlds,*
>
> *the universes.*
>
> *We created all life,*
>
> *all beings, all things*
>
> *with love.*

Yvonne immediately recognized the Shariyat by white light glowing around it.

Sometime later, in a second contemplation, Yvonne asked Towart if she could return with him to this sacred volume of the Shariyat. This time, when they came to the white light, Yvonne heard the following words flow gently into her heart:

> *Love is the only thing*
>
> *worth speaking or*
>
> *writing.*
>
> *Love is the key*
>
> *to understanding all things.*
>
> *Loving ourselves*
>
> *is our gift to God.*
>
> *Gratitude for his love*
>
> *to us.*
>
> *There is only us.*
>
> *We are all holy.*
>
> *Self-Realization is*
>
> *knowing and living,*
>
> *remembering*
>
> *who we are . . .*
>
> *The Mahanta,*
>
> *the Ancient One,*
>
> *returns again and again*
>
> *in one body or another*
>
> *to show us love,*
>
> *to remind us*
>
> *of who we are.*

———

*This time,
when they
came to the
white light,
Yvonne heard
words flow
gently into
her heart.*

———

Yvonne was learning firsthand from Towart Managi about the spring waters of golden wisdom to be found in the Shariyat in the higher worlds. She'd seen something more. Divine love, she learned, originates on the inner planes and then echoes in the world around us. Moreover, the Mahanta, the Ancient One, returns again and again to remind people of the all-encompassing love of God for them and, indeed, for all creation.

 A Spiritual Exercise to Meet Towart Managi

Sit in a quiet place, shut your eyes, then gently focus full attention on your Third Eye. It is the seat of Soul in the physical body. Its location is in the center of the head, behind and between the eyebrows. This Third Eye is also called the Spiritual Eye and serves as a window between our physical world and the worlds of God beyond.

Now, softly chant the word *aum.* It is a passkey to gain access to the Mental Plane. After a while, you may expect to hear the murmuring sound of running water. Ask ECK Master Towart Managi to take you to the Shariyat-Ki-Sugmad on the Mental Plane.

The Shariyat may appear to you as a book, a field of glowing white light, or even as heavenly music or magnificent images of some kind. However it reveals itself, be sure to open your heart to God's love. Then, simply enjoy the divine message it imparts to you.

Ask ECK Master Towart Managi to take you to the Shariyat-Ki-Sugmad on the Mental Plane.

The ECK Masters find all kinds of ways to bring the golden wisdom of ECK into your life. So always live in love, joy, and expectation. Learn the wonders of God's love that lie in store for you.

Yaubl Sacabi (*YEEOW-buhl sah-KAH-bee*) was the ECK Master among the Mycenaeans (invaders of Greece between 2000–1700 BC). He was the leading figure among the Greek mystery cults and is now the guardian of the Shariyat-Ki-Sugmad, the sacred book of ECK, in the spiritual city of Agam Des, home of the Eshwar-Khanewale, the God-eaters.

8
Guardian of the Shariyat-Ki-Sugmad at the Spiritual City of Agam Des
YAUBL SACABI

*Y*aubl Sacabi is an ECK Master many seekers would like to know more about. He is a robust man of about average height, a sturdy specimen in a physical sense. He served as the Mahanta, the Living ECK Master among the ancient Greeks soon after the arrival of the Mycenaeans and helped establish the mystery schools.

The Mycenaeans were an Indo-European group that spoke an early form of Greek. It was an ideal time for Yaubl Sacabi to appear on the scene to serve his mission, for the Mycenaeans had brought new ideas in art and architecture, so he was able to encourage their creative ventures. His influence would, in centuries to come, lead to the rise of a far more advanced Greek civilization.

Today he heads the Temple of Golden Wisdom in the spiritual city of Agam Des, in the Hindu Kush of central Asia.

Yaubl Sacabi is an ECK Master many seekers would like to know more about.

A Friend for Life

Jenny was only seven when she had her first experience with the ECK Master Yaubl Sacabi. This was years before she heard of the ECK teachings. She'd often felt useless, unloved, and unwanted until the night the ECK Master Yaubl Sacabi appeared to her in a dream.

Jenny became aware of standing beside Yaubl in a desert near a small trader's encampment. A dust storm swept in; people scurried for shelter. Nearby she spotted a little man trying to get stubborn camels to move, but they refused to stir. He cursed them roundly. When that failed to work, he cursed his son.

"Where's that useless son, Yaubl?" he shouted.

Then muttering to himself, he said, "I hoped he would take over the family business and make something of himself. But he's always off with his head in the clouds."

Seven-year-old Jenny cringed as she listened to Yaubl Sacabi's father calling him useless. Yaubl turned to her and said, "Everything I have, I will always give to anyone who needs it." Not till years later did she read a similar thought in *The Shariyat-Ki-Sugmad:* "Give the ECK Master all that you have, and he will give you all he possesses!"

The sentiment made a strong connection for her. She understood he would help her understand what her dreams meant and much more besides.

The girl looked up at the sturdy, rugged, but

Jenny had her first experience with Yaubl Sacabi years before she heard of the ECK teachings.

kindly ECK Master. He towered over her. A bald head, broad face, and squared shoulders lent the very appearance of strength, quite a different being from the youth whose father had once railed so mightily against him. After that first dream meeting, Yaubl would speak to her many times during childhood in the dream state, but it was always above the noisy background of his father's angry scolding. It was in those stormy settings that Yaubl Sacabi gave the spiritual wisdom of ECK (Holy Spirit) to Jenny, who felt useless and unwanted.

A bald head, broad face, and squared shoulders lent the very appearance of strength.

On the inner planes, ECK Masters appear to people in a way they can understand, to offer the wisdom of the ages.

Journey into Time

Days, weeks, months, and years flipped by like a staid book's pages dancing before the playful breath of an impish wind. And so it was that Jenny grew up.

In due time, she became a member of Eckankar and began to study *The ECK Dream 1 Discourses.* Soon after she tried the spiritual exercise in the first discourse, she heard the stirring sound of a drumbeat. It came not only during her contemplations, but also in her outer life. An unusual kind of flute music accompanied the drumbeat.

Flute music and a drumbeat are but two of many expressions of the holy Sound Current—the Voice of God, the Holy Spirit. This Sound is one way the Holy Spirit, the ECK, speaks to mankind.

It was around the same time that Jenny's son received an audiocassette of synthesized music. The first time she heard it, a flute playing in an oddly familiar way caught her full attention. Its music suggested ocean waves confiding secrets to a willing shore. The melody was very like one she'd once heard in contemplation after beginning *The ECK Dream 1 Discourses*.

When that haunting piece had finished playing, another began.

This selection resounded with an oddly familiar drumbeat. She shut her eyes and listened carefully. The drumbeat soon transported her into a deep state of contemplation, where once more she met her childhood teacher. It was her friend, Yaubl Sacabi.

On this occasion, he lifted her into the far reaches of outer space. Absolutely nothing was visible in the emptiness except for a single thing, a mountain ledge. Then she spotted tall, thin, pale men striding back and forth along a narrow pathway at its daunting heights. She sensed that they were masters.

An object appeared. It resembled a colossal sundial with cogwheels and gears of king-size proportions.

There, suspended in space, in a place one would need to fly in order to reach, an object appeared. It resembled a colossal sundial with cogwheels and gears of king-size proportions. Every now and again, one of the masters would leave the ledge to make an adjustment to this object. He'd simply abandon the security of the rocky shelf and walk toward this assembly of cogwheels, and, like magic, a rock would appear under his feet to step upon. The greatest wonder of all was how the rock remained firmly in place until he'd crossed the empty space, made an adjustment to the time gears, and then had returned safely to the ledge.

Jenny was within a few months of her Second Initiation. (Years ago, when I was approaching the Second Initiation, Yaubl had shown me this very same mechanism.) Yaubl Sacabi explained to her, "This is where the time of the universe is kept."

Then rose the throb of a steady drumbeat, much like the one on her son's audiocassette. It escaped from the clock.

"It sounds like the drumbeat on a Roman galley," she observed.

In the next moment, she was aboard an early Roman warship. A tall, strong man with reddish hair and beard, and dark, sunken eyes sat on a bench below deck. Her first look at the scene was from somewhere above the galley, but an instant later found her inside the very skin of that man.

She was now him!

All his thoughts and feelings became Jenny's. He—she—was a captive, set to work as an oarsman.

Jenny was seeing and reliving a past life. But why?

Yaubl Sacabi explained, "This is where the time of the universe is kept."

Jenny's Lessons from a Past Life

The first thing to strike her was the awful stench. It was a musty and sweaty odor, as one could expect from the bodies of oarsmen below deck, who rowed and rowed without end. The only light below deck slipped in from the holes where oars jutted. Through those very same oar holes, however, there burst a frigid ocean spray. It was a cold, dark, and miserable life.

No hope whatever shone in the sunken eyes of this creature she'd once been. And the thirst! It was overwhelming. Nevertheless, rather than beg the cruel overseer for water, he labored on until the overseer's replacement would come on duty. But until then, the ruthless overseer strode along the deck's walkway. The very sight of him inspired a flash of overwhelming hatred and helpless anger. The overseer was different in appearance than her husband in this lifetime, but Jenny knew in that instant the two were one and the same.

A few days later, it happened that her husband saw her absorbed in an ECK discourse. Not a member of Eckankar, he asked, "Well, what are they trying to teach you now?"

"They're trying to teach me how not to hate you!" she exclaimed. The truth of her instinctive reply struck her by its unerring accuracy.

Few people come to understand the reason they have entered into certain relationships.

Few people come to understand the reason they have entered into certain relationships. On the surface, Jenny's marriage was a good one. Her husband didn't abuse her; nor did he act like an overseer. But between them existed an opposition, an unrelenting tension. It was a stubborn carryover from the past.

What Jenny failed to note from her past-life experience were the many lifetimes in which she'd played the role of an overbearing master; and her husband, the unenviable role of subject. Yet time lends each of us a chance to resolve the evil deeds recorded in our book of life.

So Yaubl Sacabi let her revisit the past to review key karmic experiences.

More to ECK than Experiences

Yet way back when she'd been a child, she hardly understood the deep spiritual significance of her inner experiences. For example, the first time Jenny heard the Sound of God, she feared she was losing her mind.

Some people in her Satsang class have said, "I'd do anything to have your experiences."

But she's quick to reply, "Experiences are not why I stay in ECK. I stay because of the understanding I'm gaining through the ECK teachings of what those experiences mean."

ECK Masters like Yaubl Sacabi will help all who want the gift of spiritual understanding.

ECK Masters like Yaubl Sacabi help all who want the gift of spiritual understanding.

Yaubl Sacabi's Dream of Destiny

Legend has it that Yaubl Sacabi once dreamed about the destiny of the human race.

This dream came to him as a young man, some time before he found the actual teachings of ECK. One night a magnificent, shining being appeared to him. It was none other than the illustrious Sat Nam, the great being manifested in the first of the spiritual worlds. He is the mighty ruler on the Soul Plane. His purpose in coming to see

Yaubl Sacabi was to reveal to him the destiny of mankind.

Sat Nam tried to keep it simple for the neophyte.

America, he said, would enter its golden age during the final years of the twentieth century, and this peak of achievement would last for much of the twenty-first century. Then it would begin to wind down, and another civilization would rise in its stead.

It was this prophetic dream that encouraged Yaubl Sacabi to embark upon an earnest quest for the ECK teachings. And he found them. They were to help him develop undreamed-of talent and satisfaction.

The unleashing of his creative powers eventually led to a bold venture—the founding of the great spiritual city of Agam Des, tucked away in a supraphysical spot somewhere in the harsh Hindu Kush Mountains. *Agam Des* means "inaccessible world." All who wish to go there must travel in the Soul body; access is by invitation alone.

Today, Yaubl Sacabi is chief instructor at the Golden Wisdom Temple in Agam Des.

Today, Yaubl Sacabi is, of course, guardian and chief instructor at Gare-Hira, the Golden Wisdom Temple in Agam Des. It has developed into a center of spiritual culture. On display in Gare-Hira is the second section of the Shariyat-Ki-Sugmad, the Way of the Eternal—ancient and most holy scriptures of ECK. Yaubl Sacabi stands to become a central figure in the next era of human destiny.

Fortune smiles on everyone who knows him. His mission is to help seekers escape the tiresome cycles of karma and reincarnation, and find spiritual freedom.

What Is the Temple of Gare-Hira?

Gare-Hira is the fourth major Temple of Golden Wisdom on the physical plane. It lies secluded in the remote Hindu Kush, in the spiritual city of Agam Des, and is where Yaubl Sacabi is guardian and teacher. This city is also home to the Eshwar-Khanewale. Called God-eaters, they consume cosmic energy much as we do food.

The Temple of Gare-Hira is a white structure somewhat like an Islamic mosque, a sturdy building with a white dome topped by a cupola. Classrooms ring the main sanctuary. And lodged in this temple is the second section of the Shariyat-Ki-Sugmad, displayed upon the altar of the inner sanctum. The title of this section is "The Records of the Kros." As already stated, the ECK Master Yaubl Sacabi is the head teacher here, and students come nightly, by invitation, in their Soul forms, to study the ancient wisdom of God.

Students come nightly, by invitation, in their Soul forms, to study the ancient wisdom of God.

And what is the essence of Yaubl Sacabi's teaching? It is that the lot of each individual is to become a Co-worker with God, which brings to him the joys of wisdom, charity, and spiritual freedom.

Sara Visits Agam Des

Sara loved to read about people's experiences with Soul Travel. It was fascinating how the ECK Masters would meet neophyte travelers in their dreams and take them to a Temple of Golden Wisdom. She'd read many such stories in the ECK books and publications.

Sara practiced the Spiritual Exercises of ECK every day. She eagerly looked forward to having her own experiences within the grand universes of creation.

One day in contemplation, she arrived at a room that looked a bit like an ancient chapel. Three long, low steps at the front of the room led up to an alcove underneath a large marble arch, beyond which stood a lectern, with an open book upon it.

Sara's eyes grew large. This might be a Temple of Golden Wisdom and that open book upon the lectern the famed Shariyat-Ki-Sugmad.

Sara's eyes grew large. There was a strong possibility that this place might be a Temple of Golden Wisdom, and that the open book upon the lectern was the famed Shariyat-Ki-Sugmad. What an amazing find!

Early on in Sara's childhood, her mother was the organist in the church where her father was pastor. So she often enjoyed a free run of the church during the week, while her parents went about church office business. It was an opportunity she used to full advantage. She explored all the areas off limits to parishioners, venturing into every nook and cranny. In fact, such explorations also became a favorite pastime whenever the family drove to other churches in other towns where her parents had business.

Sara was, in a real sense, looking for God in the secret places in houses of worship.

So now here she was in a contemplative experience about to run up some steps to read from the

Shariyat-Ki-Sugmad, the holy book of ECK.

But something caught her eye.

High above the steps, on the marble archway, there was strange writing. It was in the script of a language she'd never heard or seen, featuring unusual marks like those of some ancient hiero-glyphics. Sara had a haunting feeling that she instinctively understood its meaning.

A weight of unhappiness dropped upon her, because the message said, "Please do not come up here unless you have been invited."

Unwilling to give in so easily, Sara considered the situation. She began to rationalize along these lines: *I'm just a new chela in ECK. Nobody's told me that's what it says. How could I know that language? And who's there to ask? I have no way to prove that it says, "Please don't come up here unless you have been invited."*

Sara knew that the precious books of the Shariyat-Ki-Sugmad contain the wisdom of the ages—the secrets of ECK that she so longed to embrace. She desperately wanted to approach the lectern.

She'd heard somewhere that its books tell the story of Soul's many lives on earth and in the other worlds, and also of Soul's spiritual unfold-ment on Its travels home to God. Sara also knew that if she was this close to an open volume of the Shariyat-Ki-Sugmad, it was possible there would be some wisdom in it pertaining to her own life's story.

How could she pass up such a golden oppor-tunity?

She'd heard that its books tell the story of Soul's many lives on earth and in the other worlds.

Disappointment welled up within her. Yet she realized it would do well to obey the precept. At the same time, however, she felt a warm and loving grace lull her troubled mind.

Then a thought flashed in her mind: God had spoken to her! And even better, she'd heard and understood. It had whispered through the knowing voice in her heart. Without the least hesitation, she'd actually grasped the meaning of the strange script. She'd instinctively known what it said. While she stood pondering the divine benevolence, a bald man in a short white robe appeared off to one side of the alcove, beneath the arch. Sara recognized him. It was the ECK Master Yaubl Sacabi. A most beautiful, mellow golden countenance and extraordinary brown eyes smiled in greeting. His eyes were warm and electric. He motioned her to mount the steps and enter the alcove. There, Yaubl Sacabi began to teach her the secrets of how to commune with the sacred scriptures.

ECK Master Yaubl Sacabi's golden countenance and extraordinary brown eyes smiled in greeting. His eyes were warm and electric.

The real lesson of the day?

Sara realized that if she had ignored the feeling of knowing the proper thing to do and had gone uninvited to read the sacred book, she would not have understood the language in the holy Shariyat. Its message would have remained a secret. She would have come without the key: a heart that was ready to hear the Master's voice. She had come within a hairbreadth of throwing away a priceless opportunity. So close, so close. And Sara learned something else too. She needed to guard everything she would learn in the future and treat it as if it were a treasure of unimaginable value.

Guardian of the Shariyat-Ki-Sugmad
at the Spiritual City of Agam Des   145
Yaubl Sacabi

Such, then, is one of the lessons that leads to wisdom, freedom, and boundless love. And Yaubl Sacabi had introduced her to it on that very special day.

Who Is Yaubl Sacabi?

In the remote, hidden spiritual city of Agam Des, Yaubl Sacabi is guardian of the portion of the Shariyat-Ki-Sugmad found there. The city is also home to the Eshwar-Khanewale, a mysterious brotherhood known as the God-eaters, because they consume cosmic energy instead of material food. It is the reason they live to ages well beyond the average span of life.

Entrance to the city, you recall, is by invitation alone, and then only in the Soul body.

You will recognize Yaubl at first sight, for his bald head looks a bit like a brass dome. A strong nose, thick neck, and well-developed muscles in arms and chest outline a capable, rugged appearance. And you soon find that he takes great pleasure in teaching you and others the secret laws of life, which give new meaning to our existence here.

He takes great pleasure in teaching you and others the secret laws of life, which give new meaning to our existence here.

Food Like a Mother's Milk

Kate was traveling to Agam Des with the Mahanta to meet Yaubl Sacabi during a spiritual exercise. She'd found Yaubl in a grass hut.

The inside of the hut was fragrant, and the high vibrations of God's love caused the very air to quiver in delight. The atmosphere was soothing and relaxed. Kate lay down on a cot she found there, and Yaubl fed her by spoon. The food was fully nurturing; she'd never tasted better.

Is this God food? she wondered.

Kate knew that the value of this food reached far beyond her understanding, like a babe loving the milk of its mother. She felt spiritually awakened. She realized that Yaubl Sacabi was thus also nurturing her awareness, as Soul, of the God Worlds of ECK.

Close, but Not Too Close

Bob, a Second Initiate for a year, made a request in his spiritual journal before the annual ECK Worldwide Seminar: Would the Mahanta take him to a Temple of Golden Wisdom?

That very same night, in a dream, he found himself walking toward a distant ECK Master, a bald man dressed in a navy blue suit. Neither spoke as Bob drew near, words being unnecessary. His first glimpse of the ECK Master filled Bob's entire being with a sweet love such as he had never, ever known.

His first glimpse of the ECK Master filled Bob's entire being with a sweet love such as he had never, ever known.

Slowly Bob strode on past him, his eyes never wavering from the face of one who could waken such peace and bliss with his mere presence alone. For all that, Bob couldn't approach closer to him than twelve or fifteen feet.

Then Bob understood the reason. He simply wasn't spiritually ready to receive more of the divine love pouring through that powerful channel of God. For Bob realized then that only when one becomes a refined channel for ECK does he become a clearer instrument of love for all God's children.

So, too, only when Bob himself became more refined in nature would he be spiritually ready to enjoy the closer company of the Adepts of the Vairagi Order.

With a Little Help from His Friends

Here's a follow-up to Bob's story:

Bob's happiness lingered long after he rolled from bed the next morning. Somehow, he knew, he would learn the name of that mighty ECK Master at the ECK Worldwide Seminar.

And, indeed, his hunch paid off. There, displayed in the bookroom, was a sketch of Yaubl Sacabi, his dream visitor.

Ever since that first occasion, Bob has longed for a second meeting with him, but he's come to realize that Yaubl Sacabi has always been by his side since the night of that dream. In fact, the Mahanta, Yaubl, and other ECK Masters will accompany him on his journey to God-Realization. Bob may, with their help, pursue his spiritual mission on earth and win spiritual freedom.

Yaubl Sacabi's presence alone inspires a spiritual call to excellence.

Yaubl Sacabi's presence alone inspires a spiritual call to excellence.

So what is the primary lesson for you in Bob's experience with Yaubl? It is to give love without condition to all God's children. Sooner or later, all will learn to do so and thus enter the heart of God.

Alice and the Beautiful City

In contemplation, Alice asked for proof that she was getting a helping hand from the ECK Masters. She, moreover, wanted evidence of spiritual progress.

So one day during a spiritual exercise, Alice met the Mahanta and asked for help in lifting the restrictions that held her back from Soul Travel. The Master called her attention to a clear, plasticlike sheath around her. As she watched, he let the sheath crack and peel away, and as it did, she felt the unmistakably sweet breath of freedom sweep in as old mind-sets fell into a heap at her feet.

The scene shifted.

Now she was on a path with the Mahanta, enjoying a landscape of magnificent mountains in the far-off distance, and a city too. Then, in front of her on the path, another ECK Master appeared. Of rugged build, he wore a short maroon robe and sturdy sandals with wide straps that protected his feet. *His dark eyes look a bit Asian,* she thought.

Alice immediately recognized Yaubl Sacabi. The city was certainly Agam Des.

She followed the Mahanta and Yaubl over a long, steep path that meandered up a grand hill toward the city. The city's beauty stole her breath. Then, at a lookout point, Alice began to feel overwhelmed by its high spiritual vibrations. She asked the ECK Masters, "Is there anything I can do to regain my balance and come into harmony with the flow of ECK here?"

By way of reply, Yaubl handed her a round, flat pan with crumbs and seeds. She could feed the

An ECK Master appeared. Of rugged build, he wore a short maroon robe and sturdy sandals with wide straps that protected his feet.

birds. This loving deed of service would restore her spiritual equilibrium.

Their small party moved on. Alice could hear a singer's high note ride upon the air. Small bells chimed. Sometimes a flute played a haunting melody. The sky glowed like a sapphire and looked down serenely on all beneath it.

The Mahanta and Yaubl began a conversation inside a building with two white domes, one behind the other. Inside one dome was what looked like a stone altar. The Shariyat-Ki-Sugmad rested upon it, looking like a bright glow of light. She stepped into this glow, gazed into the dazzling light, and wondered exactly how to go about reading the Shariyat, this holy book of the ancients.

In answer, three quick images flitted past her mind's eye: "Love thy brother and returned to you will be the Sugmad's divine love. Live in green pastures. Hallow the spiritual."

These three messages formed a perfect, clear picture for her. Here was the proof she'd wanted of the ECK Masters' assistance, and it further gave an indication of her spiritual progress that she'd asked to see.

Here was the proof she'd wanted of the ECK Masters' assistance.

And so it came about that divine wisdom entered her heart directly through the light of the Shariyat-Ki-Sugmad itself.

A Vision of the Future

Julie, an ECK chela, once declared a desire to receive the wisdom of the ECK Masters. So one weekend, while visiting someone in the Rocky Mountains of Colorado, she felt inspired to try a spiritual exercise as the curtain of evening fell. She wished for a clear vision of a situation that bothered her. She further wanted to know the future, because her life was a bit off track. In what seemed a heartbeat, she was sitting in a white tepee, in the company of someone she took to be an Indian guide.

He handed her a white arrow. She notched it in a bow, and, like magic, the arrow transformed in appearance. Its whole length was suddenly studded with emeralds, rubies, and other precious gems, and the arrowhead itself was of the most dazzling crystal. Julie let fly the arrow. But she kept one hand firmly on the bow, while with the other she clutched the arm of the Indian guide, who cradled Sinbad, her black cat. The swift arrow winged its way to its mark at Agam Des.

Then Julie had an illuminating experience, a vision, of her future self as an ECK Master.

Then Julie had an illuminating experience, a vision, of her future self as an ECK Master. A stream of love and compassion poured forth from her for the very gift of life. How precious it truly was.

This vision of the future offered a compelling insight into her present troubles as well as lending courage for the spiritual journey that would occupy the rest of her lifetime.

Within the week, she would receive the *Mystic World*, a special publication for members of Eckankar. The title on the front-page article read, "How to Become an ECK Master."

She wasted no time in trying a new spiritual exercise. Yes, Julie was on track.

Yet a question niggled at her peace of mind:

Who was that Indian guide? Later, she would be able to deduce from the following experience, and many others like it over time, that the Indian guide was Yaubl Sacabi in disguise.

Now, on with Julie's second experience that same night.

Make a Better Choice

Julie's second experience began with a pleasant walk along a familiar path lined with ancient trees, a wonderful fragrance of flowers teasing the air. She entered an old brownstone monastery on a hillside and sat down to listen to ECK Master Yaubl Sacabi address a class. He greeted her by name. He told the class that she'd offer her own story in a few minutes.

Yaubl was telling of the enormous danger of white magic, even of dabbling in it. He pointed out that when someone thinks he's above another, it is a kind of white magic, too, and has consequences. Then he turned to Julie and invited her to tell her story.

Yaubl pointed out that when someone thinks he's above another, it is a kind of white magic and has consequences.

Julie told of a recent incident that'd happened at the airport. It was certainly not a flattering story, but it did contain a graphic example of what it may sometimes take to learn humility.

She'd been at the departure gate applying for a standby seat. It appeared she was first in line for one because she'd charmed the ticket agent with dazzling smiles and shameless flattery. Mission accomplished! Julie then sat down to wait for the other passengers to board the plane.

To her dismay, another attractive woman glided up to the counter at the departure gate and threw her captivating charms at the agent. He gave her the only available standby seat—Julie's. Julie was crushed. She'd come in second in what appeared for all the world to be little more than a beauty contest, a competition for big egos. And she'd lost.

When she'd finished her story, Yaubl Sacabi addressed a thoughtful class.

"When one places all desires and all conditions into the white light of ECK," he said, "and lets the Mahanta guide one's life, that person's life will roll forward more beautifully than one could ever imagine."

Yaubl soon dismissed the class, except for Julie. "You know what is holding you back, don't you?" Yaubl asked.

"You know what is holding you back, don't you?" Yaubl asked.

Julie knew the answer before he'd said the word: anger. Anger was holding her back spiritually. She asked him how could she release the tight grip it had on her.

With surprise, she heard him say, "The answer is so simple that many overlook it: humor. A sense of humor. Good, sincere humor keeps you on the middle path. Situations where genuine humor is used cancel anger!"

Gems of wisdom like the one above are stepping-stones to fulfilling a vision of yourself as a greater spiritual being.

Long ago, Yaubl Sacabi had offered a similar bit of wisdom to a young protégé, Rebazar Tarzs, later to become an esteemed ECK Master too. "Let my spirit dwell in you," Yaubl had said. "And so shall the Sugmad (God) be exalted so that you will bear the harvest of good deeds."

He meant, of course, to allow the Holy Spirit into your life. It would crowd out all base passions, leaving only noble thoughts, words, and deeds as testimony to your new state of consciousness.

 A Spiritual Exercise to Meet Yaubl Sacabi

Before sleep, shut your eyes and sing HU, the love song to God. Do it several times.

Then imagine you're walking along an easy mountain path. The sky is a sparkling blue above you, and the sun's kisses warm the air that lingers all around you.

Now, look ahead. The path branches off in two directions. The ECK Master Yaubl Sacabi waits at one branch of it. Go with him. Ask him any question you might have about the city of Agam Des or the Temple of Gare-Hira, where the Shariyat-Ki-Sugmad rests upon a sort of reading table, or altar.

Let him lead you there.

Finally, go to sleep in peace, for all good things will come to you in due time. Be patient. Try again if the spiritual exercise shows no apparent results the first few times. Take your time. All notable things take time and effort to achieve.

The mountain path branches in two directions. ECK Master Yaubl Sacabi waits at one branch of it.

Do the above spiritual exercise before going to bed at night. In the morning, write a note in your journal about any dream or portion of a dream you may recall. The ECK Masters are always looking for the exceptional Souls by whose spiritual light the Masters will know them.

The Spiritual Exercises of ECK brighten the light of Soul. So it pays to do them.

Rami Nuri (*RAH-mee NOO-ree*) is the ECK Master who is guardian of the holy book, the Shariyat-Ki-Sugmad, on the Pinda Lok (physical world), at the House of Moksha, Temple of Golden Wisdom in the city of Retz, Venus. The letter *M* appears on his forehead.

9
Teacher at a Golden Wisdom Temple on Venus
RAMI NURI

On my early days as a student of Eckankar, I often paid visits to different Temples of Golden Wisdom like the one on Venus. It was there that I met this wonderful ECK Master. He's instructed thousands of truth seekers in the ancient scriptures of ECK.

Journey to Moksha

One night I woke outside the body. I lived in town at the time, some miles from the Wisconsin farm where I grew up. But it was on the farm that I found myself in the Soul body, hovering like a soft glow of light by the woodshed.

Suddenly there came a gentle but persistent tugging. To my astonishment, I sailed high into the sky at a breathtaking speed, and the farm rapidly fell away below me. Soon the countryside lay spread out for miles in every direction: all of Wisconsin and Lake Michigan, a mere puddle of water. And I flew higher still. My view now encompassed the entire United States, Canada, Mexico, and the vast oceans on either side.

What on earth—well, in heaven—was going on? I was to learn very soon.

Yet for some odd reason, there was no fear. A sense of calm expectancy soothed me as a mysterious force guided me even faster through the midnight veil of outer space.

On and on I soared. The blackness of eternal night hung thick all around, except for the ball of light that I was as Soul. Soon then followed a slackening of velocity. What would cap this incredible journey?

Suffused light began to paint in the inky space around me. All movement stopped.

Looking about, I found myself in a celebrated Temple of Golden Wisdom. This, I would later discover, was the House of Moksha, the Temple of Golden Wisdom in the city of Retz, Venus. Here was kept the third section of the famed holy scriptures of ECK, the Shariyat-Ki-Sugmad, "the Way of the Eternal."

The building was a translucent dome. Soft light flowed in through some kind of glass. An ECK Satsang class was in session, taught by a rather tall man with snow-white hair and short beard of matching color and sheen. It was none other than the great ECK Master Rami Nuri. He teaches people who travel there in the dream state, and who have a great longing to find the high worlds of God.

I joined the others, selecting a cushion and sitting down in back of the room. Then I listened

An ECK Satsang class was in session, taught by a rather tall man with snow-white hair and short beard of matching color and sheen.

spellbound. Rami Nuri was revealing age-old secrets and mysteries that have confounded the brightest and best religious minds of earth—on existence, other dimensions, the nature of Soul, and the like.

My Soul Travel adventure had been hard won by sticking with the Spiritual Exercises of ECK, but it was worth all the effort, discipline, love, and devotion to the Spirit of Being.

It should be said that the Mahanta, the Living ECK Master will guide anyone to the House of Moksha who is prepared to receive the wisdom to be found there. The Master, you see, is the actual passkey to get one by the guardians of the gate. Paul Twitchell was the Mahanta, the Living ECK Master then, so it was he who had accompanied me in Soul form to Earth's sister planet Venus.

Rami Nuri was revealing age-old secrets and mysteries that have confounded the brightest and best religious minds of earth.

The House of Moksha means "house of liberation." It is cloaked to human eyes because its high vibrations place it at the uttermost edge of physical matter, and it is thus only visible to those with the spiritual eyes to see. The ECK Master in charge of it is the incomparable Rami Nuri. Other ECK Masters assist him in teaching the Shariyat-Ki-Sugmad to all who come.

Who Is Rami Nuri?

Rami Nuri is a tall, well-built man whose neatly trimmed beard adds to a noble countenance. His milk-white hair is brushed back; his eyes have a lustrous sheen like anthracite. An earlier life as a mystic of the Magi during the first century before Christ marks him with more or less Oriental features.

He teaches the gospel of salvation, which can free a fettered Soul from the rounds and rounds of birth and death. So he holds forth the way to the ECKshar, the high state of consciousness found on the Soul Plane. One who reaches these sublime heights can know the past, present, and future for himself and others if he is willing to undertake the direct, rigid disciplines it takes to master the ECK-Vidya, ancient science of prophecy.

One who reaches these sublime heights can know the past, present, and future for himself and others if he is willing to undertake the disciplines.

Rami Nuri seldom leaves his temple residence but will occasionally make a sudden, unexpected appearance to an ECK chela, to give encouragement or an insight into some important matter.

A striking feature of the House of Moksha is the translucent dome at one end of the large temple complex. Again, this spiritual site is a supraphysical one; it exists well above the normal range of human perception.

Dion's Surprise Visitor

Within the first years of her ECK study, Dion made a special trip to the Temple of ECK in Chanhassen, Minnesota. This is a Golden Wisdom Temple on the physical plane where people may come to hear more about the teachings of ECK, to meet others of like mind, and to begin their journey home to God.

An ECKist at the temple introduced her to an audiobook of *The Shariyat-Ki-Sugmad*. It was a reading of the ECK bible.

Dion had been studying the holy scriptures of ECK back in Des Moines, Iowa, where she'd joined a discussion class. Once a month, she met with other members to share insights and air questions.

Soon after, she began to listen to the audiocassettes and follow along in her book, underlining things of special significance and making notes as the tape rolled on.

It was certainly a gratifying study, with all the pages and pages of spiritual knowledge this book contains.

A deep study like Dion's is actually a spiritual exercise, the true contemplation of the ECK works. It opens a student to the ever-present guidance of the ECK Adepts as the heart opens to truth.

Dion found this study an extraordinary experience.

At the end of the last tape of *The Shariyat*, as she was finishing the book, Dion's inner vision opened, and she was astonished to see Rami Nuri right there in the room with her. She deeply appreciated this blessing, for it was his special acknowledgement of her devoted study of *The Shariyat-Ki-Sugmad*.

Dion's inner vision opened, and she was astonished to see Rami Nuri right there in the room with her.

Dion's acceptance of the deeper ECK teachings has raised her state of consciousness. In telling her story, she reflected on her time in ECK. Life is becoming an ever-greater joy.

Higher Education

Chris, an ECK initiate from Australia, was a

regular attendee at a Satsang class in the city of Retz via his spiritual exercises. He'd found the Golden Wisdom Temple, the House of Moksha with its domed roof, in a breathtaking city of light near a large body of water. *Moksha* means a spiritual release from our lower bodies.

Chris was a regular attendee at a Satsang class in the city of Retz via his spiritual exercises.

There he met the ECK Master Rami Nuri, who welcomed him to class.

He'd been a regular ever since.

Chris enjoyed those gatherings. He recognized others in class and noted with pleasure how Rami Nuri treated them all as "aspirants of the Fifth Initiation."

Chris and the rest went to these classes to learn the responsibilities that accompany the Fifth ECK Initiation, which brings Self-Realization. It is the experience in which Soul recognizes Itself as pure Spirit. Self-Realization is a release from the limits and bonds of the human consciousness, and Soul is thereafter able to readily accept divine love into Itself.

Hard earned, this initiation is a true blessing of God. But much preparation is necessary before one is ready for this all-important opportunity. It is the intent of the Vairagi ECK Masters to help every Soul reach Self-Realization.

And so it was that Chris came to receive guidance from Rami Nuri on how to pass the tests of love that will one day usher in for him this major spiritual awakening, the ECKshar.

In his outer life Chris served as Arahata (teacher) of an ECK Satsang class. It was to help others gain spiritual truth and understanding. The great joy and upliftment he got from being with other ECK members also helped bolster his own spiritual progress. His service as a teacher would someday aid his further explorations of the God Worlds—a freedom that comes with the Fifth Initiation in ECK.

Teaching Satsang class helped him appreciate and apply the truths revealed in Rami Nuri's classes. It allowed his own training to gain a sound footing in his physical life, bringing him ever closer to his goal of Self-Realization.

As a result of his inner travels, Chris made some observations about his relationship with the Mahanta.

"The Inner Master," he says, "continues to be a great source of love, wisdom, and guidance in my life, especially when times are tough. The longer I am in Eckankar, the more I appreciate the high consciousness of the Mahanta."

Chris made a further observation. "I know I still fall back sometimes," he said, "but the joy of centering my life in Spirit is hard to describe."

Lucy's Timely Gift

As we know, one's memory of meeting an ECK Master often takes years of ripening before an individual can recognize that gift from long ago.

Lucy, an artist, decided to make an all-out effort to recall her inner travels. With that in mind, she began a series of experiments with the Spiritual Exercises of ECK. They helped her recall a

To make an all-out effort to recall her inner travels, Lucy began a series of experiments with the Spiritual Exercises of ECK.

spiritual experience of years ago when she was eighteen.

Back then, Lucy lay asleep in her family's home. An ECK Master came and roused her from bed, then led her to the living room. She knew him to be Rami Nuri; they sat beside each other on the couch. He told her it was time to get out on her own, to start a life independent of her mother and brothers. They'd become too dependent on her; it was holding them back spiritually.

Only several years later did Lucy observe the same herself, and she finally understood her dead-end situation and acted on Rami Nuri's advice. And his spiritual help had been available to her for years, since her youth.

Her conclusion: the ECK Masters are real. They play a key role in a seeker's life.

Her conclusion: the ECK Masters are real. They play a key role in a seeker's life, even if the individual is unaware of its beneficial nature.

In more recent days, Lucy had another important insight through an ECK waking dream. This is an ordinary daily occurrence with a parallel spiritual point. Here is how it happened:

Lucy discovered that the water distiller in her kitchen had overflowed. The counter and floor were swimming in water. It was a problem, you may be sure. A while later a cup overfilled, and that meant another cleanup. With the second spillage, Lucy finally caught on that the Golden-tongued Wisdom of ECK was speaking to her. There was a secret message about her creative inflow and outflow. They were unbalanced.

The realization struck her that the family situation of her teen years, like many of her challenges today, centered on issues of balance.

She saw that it was more than a coincidence to just then recall her divine guidance from Rami Nuri so long ago.

So Lucy began to look for ways to demonstrate divine love. She determined to continue with art projects that had lain neglected all too long. Yet at the same time she'd find ways to give extra love and care to her family.

Why the ECK Masters Work Together

Individualism is a byword in today's hey-look-at-me-me-me society. Yet for all its celebrated attraction, it is quite often self-serving.

So its boasted individualism is far from desirable.

Do you recall the motto of French novelist Alexandre Dumas's three musketeers: All for one, one for all? But the motto of today's individualism often amounts to "All for me, me for all." It's a consciousness turned in upon itself.

Each is the ECK, the very Spirit of Life Itself. Love is their unbreakable bond.

The ECK Masters are certainly individuals in the fullest sense of the word, the reason hardly a one goes off seeking personal glory. It's because each is the ECK, the very Spirit of Life Itself. Love is their unbreakable bond. How else could they live except in complete agreement with one another? Since all realize their mutual divine essence, their confidence in and support of one another is also absolute.

These God-Realized beings exist solely to serve the Sugmad (God) in true humility.

Thus they willingly and gladly follow the lead of the Mahanta, the Living ECK Master, for they know he is God's own anointed. It is the reason a student of ECK may report seeing both the Mahanta and another ECK Master in a spiritual experience.

Eve's Experience and What It Meant . . .

Rami Nuri teaches a section of the Shariyat to those who come by invitation to study at the Golden Wisdom Temple of Moksha. Many of his students arrive from the physical plane, and are really serious about reaching the heavenly worlds in this lifetime.

Here's a case in point: the story of Eve from Switzerland.

Eve had been trying a new technique in her spiritual exercises. First she'd ask the Mahanta for his blessings and guidance. When he appeared in response to her request, she would grasp his hand and let him lift her onto a soft white cloud. From that elevation she could see a panorama that included round mountaintops of light violet and blue.

The Mahanta was showing Eve she could indeed Soul Travel. It was simpler than she'd thought.

Now what could her experience mean?

The Mahanta was simply showing Eve that she could indeed Soul Travel. It was simpler than she'd thought. The key to her success? She'd completely opened her heart to the Inner Master. And during this whole experience his tremendous love was there, making it easy to trust him fully.

Then, too, there was the strength of her own

love. How could her strong faith but return to her a hundred times and more?

*   *   *

So how does the spiritual program of ECK manifest on the inner planes? As far as a seeker is concerned, it usually starts right here on the physical plane after some initial contact with the Mahanta, the Living ECK Master. That contact may come through reading an ad or article on Eckankar, or an ECK brochure or book. An initial contact may also be a friend's mention of the ECK or the Mahanta, the Living ECK Master.

So how does the spiritual program of ECK manifest on the inner planes?

So the spark may be anything. From that moment on, however, a seeker's spiritual life quickens. His dreams change. High teachers of ECK turn up in his dream state, teaching him the highest principles of an esoteric nature.

These guides are an advance team. They spell out for him the rudiments of ECK.

Among these inner guides may be any one or even many of the ECK Masters introduced in this book. They help one develop a greater understanding of spiritual law, and they hold classes at Temples of Golden Wisdom scattered from one end of the universe to the other.

Rami Nuri is one such ECK Master. The House of Moksha is but one of a series of way stations that help Soul reach an ever-greater level of consciousness.

These temples and ECK Masters play a unique role. They help an individual stand up and face the unknown, so he may continue the exciting journey into the higher planes of God. When he has passed all tests, he comes to the Soul Plane. There, the Mahanta takes over the main direction of his spiritual guidance and accompanies him the rest of the way into the heart of God.

So you can see that Rami Nuri and the other ECK Masters play an important role in the spiritual affairs of a seeker.

. . . And What Happened Then

Eve, as you can well imagine, knew none of this as a brand-new ECKist; it wasn't necessary. In time she'd come to learn it and all else. Her attention was on learning the Spiritual Exercises of ECK, as it should have been. When she was ready, deeper realizations of a spiritual kind would begin to happen in a natural way.

So on one occasion she met Rami Nuri, and this is how their meeting came about:

As she did her spiritual exercises one day, Eve found herself in full consciousness at a Golden Wisdom Temple.

As she did her spiritual exercises one day, Eve found herself with the Mahanta and in full consciousness at a Golden Wisdom Temple. She'd risen to the soft white cloud with the Mahanta as in the past. However, this time there was a surprise of sorts, for they'd arrived at a kind of mosque with a golden roof. An ECK Master with a beard greeted them at the door.

There was something about the high vibrations of the place that made it hard to make out his face, but she had the self-assurance to ask his name.

"Rami Nuri," he replied.

The party of three—the Mahanta, Eve, and Rami Nuri—made their way down a long hall, with Rami Nuri in the lead. They continued along a main corridor until an aisle branched off to the left. And there it was, the third section of the holy Shariyat-Ki-Sugmad.

The holy wisdom of God!

Eve had expected to find sacred text greet her eyes, but it intrigued her to find not a single visible word in the whole volume. Not one word. But there *was* something: a beautiful, strong light surged from its pages, taking her breath away.

And that was all Eve could remember of this remarkable experience.

*   *   *

The next day, Eve was prompted to fix a drink she sometimes made to cleanse her body. But this time there was a nudge to make drinking it a spiritual exercise. So with that in mind, she visualized the liquid as being the Light of ECK, watching it clean and purify her body. She noticed a great difference. The cleansing effects of the drink were many times more potent with the added visualization of spiritual light.

This was the first of the ways Eve's experience with the light of the Shariyat began to manifest in her daily routines.

This was the first of the ways that Eve's experience of the previous night with the light of the Shariyat in the House of Moksha began to manifest in her daily routines.

So what lesson did the experience at the Temple of Golden Wisdom teach her? Eve learned to appreciate the merits of directed visualization in one's day-to-day life.

In the Sandbox

Eric is an ECK youth with an adventurous spirit. It is fitting, then, that he's had so many stimulating inner experiences.

He is an ECKist who'd let things of a purely physical and material kind dictate his time and attention. It was, after all, a lot more fun to indulge in the five passions of the mind. These are familiar imps: lust, anger, greed, vanity, and an undue attachment to material things. But his life seemed to sail along anyway.

So why shake things up?

Then came his spiritual wake-up call—a car accident; it brought him to his knees. It suddenly became clear that he'd put physical interests before his spiritual journey home.

It was then that Eric decided he was done playing in the sandbox with the other kids.

Surveying all his misspent days, weeks, and months, Eric felt a deep sadness fall upon him.

This realization had come to him soon after his accident, through a past-life experience that the Mahanta showed him of a time he'd lived during the Roman Empire.

Eric was then a tall noble who'd learned of an ECK Master teaching disciples in the desert. So he went there too.

But being young, he soon grew restless. He took leave of the ECK Master and returned to Rome, where he joined the army. He so yearned for adventure! And shortly thereafter, his military unit was to tangle with a band of wild, savage barbarians. Then disaster struck. An enemy sol-

Eric let things of a purely material kind dictate his time. Then came his spiritual wake-up call.

dier caught him on the chest with a deadly spiked club. Eric was hurled to the ground, mortally wounded.

The Mahanta mercifully spared him the pain, yet he couldn't shut out the sights, emotions, and smells that hung like a foul and evil mist over the battlefield.

As he lay there dying, he felt a deep, deep sorrow. He'd failed the ECK Master. Far worse, he'd failed himself. Still today, he sometimes catches that awful feeling of a misspent life. It reminds him to attend to what's really important in this one.

So he puts his full attention on God.

Eric is determined to never again play in the sandbox of life. He wants to put this lifetime to better use. The accident and that past-life experience have combined to encourage a full commitment to eternal values, which alone bring true satisfaction and happiness in the end. He'd surely taken the Mahanta and the ECK Masters too much for granted. They were there to help him. But things would be different in the future, starting right now.

So that's where Eric stood.

With such a firm resolution in place, he actively solicited the aid of the Mahanta, the Living ECK Master and all the ECK Masters. Thereafter, his spiritual life took on a whole new direction.

And so it was that Eric met the ECK Master Rami Nuri again. They'd met once before while Eric had been doing a Spiritual Exercise of ECK,

With such a firm resolution in place, his spiritual life took on a whole new direction.

for with his newfound commitment, his experiences were coming fast, one upon another. It seems to be a corollary that the more one dedicates time to contemplation, the more frequent and matter of fact are his spiritual experiences.

That was true, in any case, with Eric.

This second meeting with Rami Nuri was certainly down to earth. Yet embedded in it was a revelation of great importance.

Here's what happened:

Eric awoke in the Soul body to the ringing of a doorbell. And there stood Rami Nuri.

Eric awoke in the Soul body to the ringing of a doorbell. And there stood Rami Nuri, whom Eric recognized only sometime later. The ECK Master held a peculiar device, long and black, a glowing light at its tip, which he touched to Eric's solar plexus the moment the door opened. Eric felt a mild shock.

Then Rami Nuri dropped something in the mailbox. He left immediately. The material said Rami Nuri was responsible for pest control. Pest control?

Back inside the house, Eric found a disgusting sight: The place was crawling with insects, scores and scores of them.

So what was the meaning of his experience?

The insects, he realized, had all come from within him and represented the whole body of attachments and frivolous things he'd been holding on to. Unfortunately, he and his dad couldn't catch the insects. They needed an expert's help.

Rami Nuri returned just at that moment. He placed a glass jar on the floor, and a light shone from the ceiling; the jar glowed.

Suddenly, as if of one mind, the insects started toward the jar and, one by one, entered it. Rami Nuri picked it up and left. What did that mean? Eric understood he was to turn over to the ECK all attachments and worries, for It would help discard them.

And so, Eric found his second meeting with Rami Nuri to be highly rewarding spiritually. He felt a sense of joy and renewal.

Eric was delighted to be away from the sandbox of life. He'd come of age.

A Step toward Freedom

Liz was another chela who once came to study the Shariyat-Ki-Sugmad in the House of Moksha. From that visit she learned the true nature of liberation, which is more than a onetime experience. It is an ongoing awakening to God's love.

Liz learned liberation is more than a onetime experience.

So Liz found herself in that particular temple during a spiritual exercise. She strolled down a long, narrow hallway, which made a sudden left turn. There she found a large, diamond-shaped opening to a room and stepped in.

The room held many seats, but it appeared she would be the only one there. At the head of the room stood a dais. Liz took a seat and waited patiently. As she sat alone in this classroom, she realized the lesson she'd receive would be specific to her needs, for there was no other person in the room.

Then Rami Nuri appeared on the dais. Via telepathy she understood his prompting—to let go of all thoughts, feelings, mind patterns, and expectations. Instead, she was to open herself to all new information, and it could be on any spiritual topic under the sun.

Behind Rami Nuri flowed a column of streaming golden white light. The Shariyat seemed to float in the midst of it. There rose then a light humming sound, so Liz shut her eyes and began to contemplate. She sang HU, the sacred name for God. And as she did so, she could hear a heavenly choir singing HU. She realized then that this supposedly empty classroom was really wall-to-wall with people. But they were invisible.

Yet they were all there, each receiving custom-made instructions as well.

During the HU Song, Rami Nuri began to speak. He read from the Shariyat. But his voice blended with the delightful, life-giving HU. And because of that blending, Liz couldn't make out the meaning of the words. She could not understand them. However, she stayed with the experience. Soon she felt her mind, emotions, and mental patterns release their grip, for she was washed clean by the sound of HU and Rami Nuri's melodic voice.

She was washed clean by the sound of HU and Rami Nuri's melodic voice.

Rami Nuri certainly had the power to liberate her spiritually, and it was as if his very atoms could teach hers by his presence alone. Liz was a far better woman in many ways after this tremendous inner experience.

For example, back in her everyday world, she noted a light happiness replacing the pull of habits upon her thoughts, actions, and feelings. They had begun to disappear. And best of all, she now welcomed change. No longer did she dread the future, for her spiritual life had entered a much larger room. This experience with Rami Nuri and the Light and Sound of God had brought Liz to a greater degree of spiritual awareness. She'd never, ever, be the same again.

She was to learn in time to come that each state of liberation delivers an intense feeling of love, joy, and freedom. The Vairagi ECK Masters are here to help every Soul gain spiritual freedom in this very lifetime.

The Tenth Door

The individuals whose stories are cited in this chapter are going through the Tenth Door. It is the road that leads to the kingdom of heaven. *The Shariyat-Ki-Sugmad,* Book 1, is the source for this knowledge.

The Tenth Door is the Spiritual Eye. It is located behind and between the eyebrows.

All the attention, says *The Shariyat,* must be withdrawn from the body and focused on the Tenth Door. Then the journey begins.

All the attention must be focused on the Tenth Door. Then the journey begins.

It is instructive to read *The Shariyat* itself on this point, for it also includes the thoughts of Rami Nuri. It reads:

> The human body does not have to die to make these journeys to God. Each visit will be only temporary until one leaves the body for the last time on earth. This is the art of death in life. The meaning of this was brought forth

when Rami Nuri, the great ECK Master in charge of the Shariyat-Ki-Sugmad in the House of Moksha in Retz, the capital of Venus, said, "He that wants life badly will never have it, but he that gives it up for the ECK, shall have all life."

This is the true meaning of the death-in-life struggle, for once life is given up to serve only the ECK, he who does so becomes blessed. Truth is manifested when one seeking God wants to be shown the supreme Deity, for he has only to look upon the Living ECK Master to fulfill this desire.

*   *   *

The following is a good seed for contemplation.

 A Spiritual Exercise to Meet Rami Nuri

To bring your vibrations into harmony with this Golden Wisdom Temple, softly sing Moksha-alayi.

First, take a comfortable position, shut your eyes, and put your full attention on the Spiritual Eye found between and behind the eyebrows.

The House of Moksha is a dome-shaped structure of a translucent material that echoes with the Sound Current of God. To bring your vibrations into harmony with this Golden Wisdom Temple, softly sing *Moksha-alayi* (MOHK-shah ah-LAH-yee) for ten or fifteen minutes.

Do all the above with a sweet love for God in your heart. This love is a magnet for your desire to meet Rami Nuri, who is a Flame of God. Your experience will be one of a kind, so stay alert.

For most people, it may take one or more attempts to meet Rami Nuri. But keep at it; you can succeed if you really want to.

Paul Twitchell was the Mahanta, the Living ECK Master from 1965 until his translation (death) from the physical plane in 1971. He introduced the modern teachings of Eckankar to the peoples of the world through his many books, lectures, and writings. His spiritual name is Peddar Zaskq.

10
American Cliff Hanger and Founder of Eckankar
PAUL TWITCHELL
(Peddar Zaskq)

Paul Twitchell raised the curtain on Eckankar in the mid-1960s and remained the Light Giver until his death in the autumn of 1971. The crowning jewel of his achievement was to quench a seeker's longing for God by putting into plain words the knowledge of divine Light and Sound. Without them, the gateway to heaven is shut.

Are You Ready?

Paul, whose spiritual name is Peddar Zaskq, came into this world with great spiritual power. Some people had already met this spiritual traveler on the inner planes years before he began his mission in 1965, while he was still in training to become the Mahanta, the Living ECK Master.

For example, Al met Paul in a dream some fourteen years prior to an actual meeting in the physical world. It happened like this:

In the dream, a stranger approached him and said, "Are you ready?" Al knotted his brows. Was

Paul, whose spiritual name is Peddar Zaskq, came into this world with great spiritual power.

this the angel of death? He certainly wasn't ready for that kind of invitation. "No thanks," he muttered. Then, fourteen years later as Al was leaving a bookstore, Paul Twitchell came up to him, took him by the arm, and asked the very same question as in the dream.

"Are you ready?"

The veil from the past snapped up like a window shade. He recognized Paul, the stranger in his long-ago dream.

Others have reported instances like this with Paul. Masters-in-training undergo many years of discipline before they are ready to accept the Rod of ECK Power. They are already High Initiates in the secret teachings of ECK before they ever enter that select circle of candidates.

Masters-in-training undergo many years of discipline before they are ready to accept the Rod of ECK Power.

Who Is Paul Twitchell?

When the ancient mysteries had strayed so far afield that only garbled fragments remained in the public mind, the Order of Vairagi Adepts decided to send forth a chosen one from among its ranks to restore truth.

In preparation, Peddar Zaskq therefore took on certain incarnations to bring about the spiritual polishing needed for Mastership. Born as Paul Twitchell in the early part of the twentieth century, he dabbled in a variety of professions. These included writer, promoter, and military man. They proved to be furnaces that would temper a rebellious nature to fit him for his mission—bringing the Light and Sound of God to people at all levels of consciousness.

A feisty man, Paul called himself a Cliff Hanger. This term evokes the image of a man hanging by his fingertips to the edge of a cliff, high above the swarming masses lost in the drudgery of day-to-day living. The Cliff Hanger can feel the high winds and is kin to the eagles, but he never dare let go.

Young Paul had enjoyed an illumination at age eight that left him ever after a rebel. Years of heartache and pain were to come and go before his life-changing experience of God-Realization in 1957. Even after that, however, life would continue to crush and squeeze him until it recast his deepest thoughts and emotions. Then and only then would he have the mature spiritual qualities needed to be the next Mahanta, the Living ECK Master. In 1965, he rose to the challenge, when Rebazar Tarzs, the Torchbearer of Eckankar, passed the Rod of ECK Power to him.

He Begins His Mission

A trail of outrageous tales surrounds this unique Master from Paducah, Kentucky, but every activity and experience from youth on was drawing him ever closer to the bosom of the ECK (Holy Spirit) to serve Its cause.

In late 1956 or early 1957 Paul had the experience of God recorded in his book *The Tiger's Fang*.

Yet, if he had truly touched the face of God as early as 1956, some may wonder why it took till

Years of heartache and pain were to come and go before his life-changing experience of God-Realization in 1957, recorded in his book The Tiger's Fang.

1965, another nine years, for him to become the Mahanta, the Living ECK Master. It's quite simple. One's habits and emotions build up over the years, and although consciousness may take the lead, the individual's emotions can take awhile to play catch-up.

If Paul ever felt like the lonely Cliff Hanger before, he must surely have felt it after his experience of God-Realization.

Paul's early efforts to present the teachings of ECK began well before he coined the words *ECK* and *Eckankar* to serve that purpose. He launched his mission at the humble roots, with weekly lectures to small groups of fifteen to thirty people at the California Parapsychology Foundation in southern California.

Paul's agenda showed how an ordinary person could move into ecstatic states of being the natural way.

In those days, Paul referred to Soul Travel as bilocation. It was, he said, the best way to reach the Supreme Oneness. He was trying to express the grandeur of the Sugmad, the Supreme Being, and taught that the way to It was through the Voice of God. We call this voice the ECK (Holy Spirit).

Paul Twitchell gave public lectures on Divine Spirit. He spelled out that it is the violation of Its laws through ignorance that binds every man, woman, and child to fear, misery, and despair. His small workshops in southern California were to introduce truth seekers to their spiritual identities. So his agenda featured a discussion of Soul. It also showed how an ordinary person could move into ecstatic states of being the natural way, without drugs. He further addressed the troubles and cares that his audience laid before him.

The topics in his presentations ranged from Spirit, or ECK (the cosmic Light and Music of God), to karma and reincarnation.

In appearance, Paul Twitchell was an unimposing man. He was of medium height and favored a business suit at public events. He was clean shaven, not bewhiskered. Yet his message startled many: Man can enter the kingdom of heaven while still living in the human body.

That was news!

Paul was learning to be his own best drumbeater as early as the 1930s. Any time he achieved the smallest thing of note, he'd fire off a flurry of press releases or letters about it. Some would call him a shameless self-promoter; however, he was picking up the art of how to catch the public's eye.

So without knowing the reason, Paul was urged to fine-tune his self-promotion. He learned to advertise himself in every possible way and in general was preparing for the future when he could turn that talent to promoting the books and articles on Eckankar and present it to the real God seekers in every corner of the world.

The ECK teachings have been here since man's earliest history, but without the name of Eckankar. They have existed under various names in different eras because of the danger of presenting the pure teachings in public. But conditions have changed today.

Thus, the ECK moves in mysterious ways to prepare future Living ECK Masters for the su-

His message startled many: Man can enter the kingdom of heaven while still living in the human body.

preme mission of all lifetimes. His case was no exception.

A Master Compiler

The high teachings of ECK had been scattered to the four corners of the earth. Different religions held bits and pieces of them, but they had attached their own conditions, or strings: they said that one had to be a vegetarian, or needed to meditate a given number of hours a day to be a true disciple of a given path to God. Many such restrictions are wrong for this day and age. Earlier teachings drawn from the original ECK works were geared for the spiritual needs of earlier cultures.

Paul collected the golden teachings scattered about the globe and rendered them into a single body of teachings readily available to all.

Paul's task was to gather the time-tested bits and pieces of the most accurate parts of what had been given in the past. In a sense, he became a master compiler.

He collected the golden teachings scattered about the globe and rendered them into a single body of teachings, that made them readily available to all. Now there's no need to hide away for ten or fifteen years in an ashram in India, sitting in the dust with buzzing flies—or, worse, locked away in a walled-up little cell to keep one's attention from the outside world—to live a better spiritual life.

The consciousness here in the twenty-first century is as valid as any in the past. People have families, jobs, recreational activities, meetings with friends after work, and, to top it off, their kids wanting a chauffeur for Little League or soccer games. It is the way of today's high-speed society.

So people today do indeed enjoy a valid state of consciousness for Soul to gain the experience It needs to find the most direct way home to God too.

That way is Eckankar.

Temple of Awesome Beauty

Some years ago, John, a soldier at a military base in the Midwest felt a persistent urge to start a dream journal. The reason was unclear, because he didn't remember his dreams. But the day he took the step of keeping a pen and notebook by his bedside, he began to recall the most vivid dreams. Dutifully, he jotted each one down.

Soon his dream experiences saw a change. They stopped being just dreams; now he was moving into the other worlds in full consciousness.

One day he reviewed the notes following his travels outside the body. There was a definite pattern. Although he now enjoyed a state of awareness greater than the dream state, he was hardly in control of this new mode of travel. Some other force was directing his inner experiences.

What could that force be?

One night while John was out of the body, a spiritual traveler paid him a visit in the Light body, also called the Nuri Sarup. It is the astral sheath, a glittering form that sparkles like millions of tiny stars. The traveler grasped his hand, and together they soared high above a grand city. His guide directed his attention below to a Temple

One night while John was out of the body, a spiritual traveler paid him a visit in the Light body, also called the Nuri Sarup.

of Golden Wisdom of such incredible beauty that tears clouded the eyes of this neophyte traveler.

There are many Temples of Golden Wisdom. Each houses a portion of the Shariyat-Ki-Sugmad, the ancient bible that contains the secret knowledge and wisdom of God's Light and Sound. These temples and works are under the guardianship of the ECK Masters.

In due course, John was discharged from service and returned to civilian life. Then, eight years later, while browsing in a bookstore, a friend selected a book on a shelf and handed it to him.

"I think you'll like this one," he said.

It was *ECKANKAR—The Key to Secret Worlds.* He took the book and turned it over to read the back cover.

There was a picture of Paul Twitchell. John instantly recognized him as the spiritual traveler who'd accompanied him to a Temple of Golden Wisdom years ago. The memory of that beautiful temple came rushing back. Finally, he understood the purpose of that experience—to serve now as a bridge to his discovery of the ECK teachings.

When the student is ready, the Master appears.

John had not been ready to become an ECKist eight years earlier. He still needed more experience. Ahead was yet the challenge of subduing his fear. Moreover, certain other preparations were also in order before he could take this big step to accept the Master's teachings.

When the student is ready, the Master appears.

The Mahanta often comes first in his radiant body, which shimmers like so many twinkling stars. Such inner experiences occur more often and with more vividness in ECK than in possibly any other spiritual path on earth, because this teaching pulses with the actual Light and Sound of God as its dynamic, living elements.

Lessons for Living

Bill told of a silver dollar given to him at age eight, when he lived on the East Coast. His parents ran a rooming house.

One day a traveler booked a cheap room. He proved to be an interesting chap, but obviously down on his luck. Billy's uncle had presented the boy with the silver dollar for his birthday. The uncle advised him to keep a sharp eye on it. Someday it would prove of great value. But Billy decided to give it to the down-and-out lodger, even though the man had never asked for money. "You need it more than I do," he declared.

Unfortunately, young Billy got in trouble for his benevolence. His mother gave him a good scolding for being so foolish when she learned he'd given the coin to the boarder. Billy felt awful.

A few weeks went by, and one night Billy had a remarkable dream. In it, the boarder held up the silver dollar. "It's very precious, isn't it?" the man asked. Billy nodded. The man then carefully placed the silver dollar into his hand. "Now hold tight," he said before disappearing.

Billy awoke. The silver dollar lay tightly clutched in his hand.

Years passed, Billy grew up, but his thoughts often returned to the mysterious reappearance of

Inner experiences occur with more vividness in ECK because this teaching pulses with the actual Light and Sound of God.

his silver dollar. What logical way might it have come back into his possession? In the end he realized the easiest thing would be to simply accept the fact that the man in his dream had restored it to him.

Years later, as a grown man, Bill became a member of Eckankar. It was shortly after Paul Twitchell's translation (passing) on September 17, 1971. When Bill saw pictures of the founder of Eckankar, he recognized him at a glance.

"That's the very same man who stayed in my parents' rooming house when I was a child," he said. "He's the man who gave me back my silver dollar in the dream!"

The Game of Life

Bill recalled other things about the lodger from his boyhood. For one, the man had often played checkers with him.

"Checkers is like the game of life," the lodger said. "I'm going to show you how to play it better."

The first time they played, the game ended before the boy knew it, because the man was a very adept player. "Checkers is like the game of life," he said. "I'm going to show you how to play it better." They set up the board and began a new game. Billy moved one of the pieces.

"Now look where you put that piece," the man said. The move looked OK to Billy.

"You moved it here because you knew what *you* wanted to do. But you also have to anticipate what I'm going to do. And now that you've taken your finger off the checker, you can't do anything else until I make my move."

"I want to show you something else," the man said. "When you moved your checker, notice how you boxed yourself into a corner." The boy studied the board. Sure enough, he was corralled. "Now you're going to have to pay the price."

Upon Billy's next move, he was forced into a position where he'd sacrifice a couple of checkers. It was the toll for not thinking ahead and leaving himself a way out.

Paul had just been passing through the area. He was then in training for the ECK Mastership, which he would achieve a few years hence. Even back then, Paul was ever the teacher.

As the Mahanta, the Living ECK Master, Paul Twitchell wanted the individuals under his care to someday become Masters too, yet how could they if he did all their thinking and work for them? He pointed out that the solution for every problem lies within our own consciousness.

Paul Twitchell pointed out that the solution for every problem lies within our own consciousness.

Rosemary's Visit from a Guardian Angel

Rosemary wrote of an experience in 1983, twelve years after Paul Twitchell's translation (death). At the time she'd owned a beautiful beach home, a duplex. Her mother, who lived in the other half, had a trailer for sale. In front of her mother's duplex was a sign, "Trailer for Sale."

One day it was raining hard. Rosemary's daughter, only two at the time, was at play on the living-room floor, so Rosemary decided to take a quick shower while her daughter was amusing herself.

Rosemary was a new member of Eckankar. She had a stack of ECK books on the coffee table; others were piled high on the refrigerator.

While in the shower, she heard a man's voice in the living room. She turned the water off, put on a towel, and went to look. There stood a strange man. "Can I help you?" she asked. It was one of those awkward moments, yet for some reason she felt no fear.

The man said, "Your daughter let me in. And I was talking to her." He said he wanted information about the trailer for sale.

"That's my mother's," Rosemary replied. "You'll have to come back tomorrow or some other time when she's here. I'm taking a shower right now, and I think it would be better if you came back another day."

To get from his car to her door, he should have been soaked, drenched. Yet he and his clothing were perfectly dry.

He agreed and turned to leave. But as he was on his way out, Rosemary noticed it was still pouring rain. Her home had no porch or any kind of landing. To get from his car to her door, he should have been soaked, drenched. Yet he and his clothing were perfectly dry.

Rosemary studied this mystery. She began to wonder about what didn't add up.

She saw him to the door, locked it, then withdrew to her bedroom to dress. She was more than ready to forget this odd experience. However, when she returned to the living room minutes later, her two-year-old took an ECK book from the coffee table. It was *The Tiger's Fang* by Paul Twitchell. The child turned it over.

There, on the back cover Rosemary saw a picture

of the very man who had just been in her living room. She exclaimed, "That was Paul Twitchell!"

But the man's been dead for twelve years, she thought. That really didn't add up.

That night Rosemary's little girl had a hard time falling asleep. She cried and fussed. Rosemary finally got up to comfort her, but the child's agitation wore on. The grandmother's consolation proved of little use either. The child wept into the wee hours.

Before returning to bed, the grandmother felt a nudge, which moved her attention to a space heater plugged into the wall. She had a sudden premonition: the heater was defective. So she unplugged it for the night. Dawn finally broke. None of the family had gained much rest, so they decided to go out for an early breakfast. While they were absent from home, the duplex burned to the ground.

The little girl had spent the whole night in tears over something. At age two she was too young to explain: "I think something very bad is going to happen because that nice man who was here today told me, and he told me in my dreams too. And that's why I'm crying."

Two-year-olds don't express themselves so well. But they can cry, and cry she did.

The fire inspector later said the cause of the fire was that faulty heater, which had been plugged in again before they left for breakfast. If the grandmother hadn't unplugged it earlier, the heater would have caught fire during the night and destroyed that old wooden building with them all

On the back cover Rosemary saw a picture of the very man who had just been in her living room. She exclaimed, "That was Paul Twitchell!"

inside. It's unlikely anyone would have escaped.
The two women realized that ECK Master
Peddar Zaskq (Paul Twitchell) was indeed very
much alive and working in the Soul body, appear-
ing to those with whom he had a close bond of
affection. The child had been with him in previous
lives. For that very reason, he'd come to protect
her. Rosemary and her family's recognition of Paul
Twitchell's intervention in a time of great danger
reaches far into the realm of unending gratitude.

The ECK Masters are guardian angels, near you all the time.

Should you ever hear me speak of opening your
wings, it means to come into an awareness of the
spiritual love and protection of the ECK Masters.

They are guardian angels, near you all the time.
Just open your awareness and rise above the
cramped arena of the human consciousness so you
can recognize and accept their benevolence.

Friend of the Family

Janice once told of an experience with Paul
Twitchell that illustrates a function of the Inner
Master. It's a role he played during the six years
he served as the Mahanta, the Living ECK Master.

At the time, Janice worked as a schoolteacher
and was staying with her mother. After arriving
home from work at night, she'd retire to her room
to contemplate and rest before grading student
papers till midnight and later.

One night when Janice came from her room, her
mother asked, "Were you just in contemplation?"

"Yes, I was."

"Well, I think your man got into the wrong

room." Janice had told her mother about Paul Twitchell, in those days the spiritual leader of Eckankar.

Her mother added, "I was just lying in bed, thinking about nothing in particular, and suddenly I saw a blue light begin to swirl in front of me. If you hadn't told me about the Blue Light of ECK, I would have thought I had glaucoma. As I watched this blue light, it formed into the face of a man."

"What did the man look like?"

"He had kind of a round German face." Being part German, the mother deemed it a pleasant enough face.

Janice went to her room to locate a picture of Paul. "That's the man," her mother exclaimed. "How could this be? I'm not even studying ECK."

Yet she had an open mind about ECK. She never criticized her daughter for being a student of ECK and was open to the Spirit of Life.

So continue with the Spiritual Exercises of ECK to open your heart to this Spirit of Life. Then you may also see the Light of God. Perhaps shortly, you'll also be privileged to hear the delightful melody of God's Voice, the ancient and holy Sound. The teachings of ECK show one how to find the presence of God.

"That's the man," her mother exclaimed. "How could this be? I'm not even studying ECK."

A Rapport with Paulji

Jeanne, an ECKist from France, had two dreams; both were with Paulji, an affectionate name for Paul Twitchell, or Peddar Zaskq. He's very much alive and active in the spiritual worlds. He often helps me today, as do many other ECK Masters.

Jeanne continues to enjoy a rapport with Paulji. In the first of her two dreams, they sat in a large room where a Satsang class was in session. (Satsang is a study of spiritual scriptures.) An ECK Master was teaching it. All the students had a discourse before them and studied it with the utmost care and attention. Jeanne did not have a discourse as did the others. All she had was a pillow.

She awoke understandably upset. *Why did everyone else have a discourse and I only a pillow?* she wondered.

Then a curtain opened and let in a tide of realization: she'd been sleeping on the job. She'd neglected her spiritual exercises. Nor had she been reading the ECK discourses, though it is the discourses that set the stage for receiving the life-giving spiritual food of love, wisdom, and knowledge. Of course, the pillow meant she had neglected her disciplines. Now she must do something about it.

Jeanne dropped into a second dream, but this one was all in black and white, not color. In it, she felt a sudden urgency to reach a certain bus stop. Paulji, as usual, was to be there at an appointed hour. She was desperate to get there. As she crossed the street to the bus stop, she happened to glance down. In her hand was a book, *The Spiritual Exercises of ECK*. Its cover was in full color even though the rest of her dream was all in shades of black and white. The cover was especially striking

Peddar Zaskq often helps me today, as do many other ECK Masters.

with its rich, magnificent tones.

Jeanne wondered about that. Why did the ECK book stand out so?

Then a rumbling noise caused her to look up just as a bus raced by. Paul was in the bus; he waved from a window. Jeanne saw him as a rather smallish man with twinkling blue eyes and a broad smile, a description that fit him to a turn.

What does this dream mean? she wondered. *Why was the whole dream in black and white but* The Spiritual Exercises of ECK *in full color?*

There were three lessons in her second dream.

First, the spiritual exercises were the colorful link between her and the ECK. Second, they gave her the means to meet the Mahanta and other ECK Masters like Paulji. Third, it's important to do the spiritual exercises at the same time every day, on schedule. In this case it meant being at the bus stop at the appointed hour.

If you want to be more in tune with communications from the Holy Spirit, set a time. Make an appointment. It is the best way to conduct prayer sessions, meditations, or contemplations.

Isn't it well worth the effort to schedule an appointment each day with the source of all life?

Jeanne saw him as a rather smallish man with twinkling blue eyes and a broad smile, a description that fit him to a turn.

Make No False Gods

An individual striving for God-Realization is to take care not to fashion the personality of the Living ECK Master into that of an idol or a personal god.

Alex, a chela from outside the United States, reported a very unsettling but instructive experience after returning home from an ECK seminar. He'd shut his eyes and gone into contemplation when Peddar Zaskq appeared before him. He was visible only from the waist up. Alex was so in awe at the unexpected appearance of this mighty ECK Master that he bowed again and again.

"Oh, I am so happy to be in thy presence, my lord," he exclaimed with overdone humility.

"Yes, yes," said Peddar Zaskq. He looked annoyed.

"Master," Alex said, "I want the blessings of God."

"My son, you shall have them," replied Peddar Zaskq. "My love is always with you. Plod on, my son, and I will help you take your country into the spiritual mainstream."

Alex felt his heart swell with love and joy. He fell to his knees again.

"Lord, may I kiss thy feet?"

The Master's feet suddenly appeared, as did the rest of his body. Just as Alex was set to kiss his foot, Peddar Zaskq disappeared, but his voice echoed from the ethers: "Call me when you're ready to get back to basics," he said.

Worship of the personality of the Living ECK Master or any ECK Master is not part of the basics.

Worship of the personality of the Living ECK Master or any ECK Master is not part of the basics. Alex did not yet understand. In his country it's the custom for a disciple to bow and kiss the feet of his Master. But it's just another way to abase ourselves, creating gods out of Masters.

People may say, "There is one who has God

Consciousness." Yet in so doing they neglect to strive for their own greater unfoldment. They are ready to accept the God Consciousness of another but then harm themselves by worshiping him, raising him in stature to what is, in fact, a false god. It is all to their undoing; they lose by it. Thus they delay the day when they, too, could stand alongside the great Masters as equals in spiritual attainment before God.

The Mission of Paul Twitchell

I once saw Paul in the library of a Temple of Golden Wisdom. He was standing in an alcove on the mezzanine level. The room was rather dark except for a shining golden light that spilled over Paul and the book on a desk before him. Paul stood reflecting.

Looking on, I recognized that only a very few understood and appreciated the gifts he'd offered through the body of writings and teachings about ECK. He expected no praise, no applause. He simply kept doing what had to be done—bringing out truth—without thanks or reward.

Paul Twitchell came to gather the scattered fragments of truth and put them in a single body of teachings. That was his mission.

Paul Twitchell came to gather the scattered fragments of truth and put them in a single body of teachings. That was his mission. It meant he had to work fast, for after a poisoning in Spain it was evident he must soon drop the physical body. The damage to it was simply too great.

He certainly had nothing to gain from continuing, yet the Holy Spirit drove him on, to gather these writings in one place. As a result, no seeker today need abandon family, job, or other responsibilities, or spend money on a personal expedition to some far-off, remote sacred location—to the Vatican library, or even to India or Tibet. There is no reason to pass one's whole life trying to track down the ancient truths revealed to mankind in hopes of advancing his own spiritual understanding.

The true teachings are here and now.

In Eckankar.

Nothing set down in any book can ever be a perfect reflection of absolute truth, however. Yet if the written word can inspire a seeker, give him a road map to heaven, shut the door on the fear of death, and release him from an overblown concern about what others might think—and so get on with this life, living in full consciousness—then Paul's mission will have been a resounding success.

Even today he loves to bring to light the hidden truths, to share them with people.

Since 1971, Paul Twitchell has moved on to a new mission, a greater challenge. Such is the bold nature of those who serve as Co-workers with God.

Yet even today as he keeps busy with any number of projects, he enjoys research and writing most of all. He loves to bring to light the hidden truths, to share them with people on all levels.

A Spiritual Exercise to Meet Paul Twitchell

As you lie in bed ready for sleep at night, picture a library on the blank screen of your mind. Imagine the library in a beautiful and serene atmosphere. Note how row upon row of books stacked on tall shelves create corridors in a rotunda filled with soft light.

Now, sing HU. It is the ancient, honored name for God. Fill yourself with Its all-giving and healing love.

Tiptoe among the stacks until you find Peddar Zaskq working at a desk, bathed in golden light. His sparkling blue eyes will greet you. Ask him to guide you to the jewels of truths hidden all around you. You may also pose a spiritual question for which you'd like the answer.

Ask Peddar Zaskq to guide you to the jewels of truths hidden all around you.

Paul Twitchell figured out the key of how to teach others to become Co-workers with God. The Spiritual Exercises of ECK as taught by the ECK Masters of the Vairagi will provide all the help you'll ever need.

They open your heart to God's love as nothing else can. Paul, through them, thus showed others the most direct route to God, the easy way.

Harold Klemp is the present Mahanta, the Living ECK Master. He received the Rod of ECK Power at midnight of October 22, 1981, in the Valley of Shangta at the Oracle of Tirmer, under the direction of Rebazar Tarzs, the Torchbearer of Eckankar. As the spiritual head of Eckankar, he brings new life and hope to thousands for a better, more direct way to God. His spiritual name is Wah Z, or Z.

11
The Mahanta, the Living ECK Master— A Modern Prophet
SRI HAROLD KLEMP
(Wah Z)

*S*ometimes I tell my wife, "I wish I were able to say things better and more clearly so people could take home with them the most spiritual benefit."

I am well aware of my limitations.

Nevertheless, there are two parts of the Master: the Outer Master and the Inner Master. In my talks and through my writings, I act in the capacity of the Outer Master, to pass along to you all I can.

The greater part of this teaching, however, is the Inner Master, the Mahanta. This state of consciousness is my inner side.

The ECK teachings are likewise of two parts: the outer and the inner. The outer teachings include my talks, books, and discourses, as well as the *Mystic World* for the members of Eckankar. But the inner teachings abide as the far greater part of this path. Among these are your actual dreams and

There are two parts of the Master: the Outer Master and the Inner Master.

dream travel, Soul Travel, and the ECK-Vidya—an insight into your future or other things of spiritual interest if an occasion warrants it.

So open your heart to Divine Spirit, the holy ECK.

This is an important point. Its eternal love takes shape in a visible being you can see inwardly as the Mahanta, the Inner Master. Each member of ECK meets him sometime or other. In seeing him, you see and hear Divine Spirit Itself. The richest of blessings come to all so fortunate as to encounter the Inner Master or some other ECK Master. It is equally true of those who catch the wonderful Light or Sound of God.

Everything of this nature is good, for it lifts you in spiritual consciousness.

First Meeting

An individual's first meeting with the Mahanta, the Living ECK Master may be quite an ordinary event.

An individual's first meeting with the Mahanta, the Living ECK Master may be quite an ordinary event, one to excite little or no interest in God. The entire occasion could well slip from his active thoughts. A seeker lets it hurry away, like just another of a hundred ants. The special moment is lost. The humdrum conditions around this meeting with the Master soon swallow all memory of it.

And the seeker's spiritual life appears to rattle on without a guiding principle in sight.

On the other hand, a greeting from the Master, the Godman, the Wayshower, may have a powerful impact, sparking a sharp reaction in the person when this spiritual being approaches him for the first time.

For example, Beth, from a U.S. Sun Belt state, tells of the time she met Wah Z in a San Francisco hotel lobby in the mid-1950s. This was some twenty-five years before he actually became an ECK Master. He handed her a copy of *ECKANKAR— The Key to Secret Worlds* by Paul Twitchell. This book would not be published until fifteen years in the future. She did not know it then.

The book challenged her beliefs. Some of it supported her philosophy, but overall it seemed of no real value.

Wah Z had not revealed his identity to her. In a very short time, therefore, all traces of this event skipped from her conscious mind, like a playful child.

It was twenty-five years later that Beth did learn his name, when she made a visit to an Eckankar meeting. There she was startled to see his picture on a book jacket—it was Wah Z, the Mahanta, the Living ECK Master. Furthermore, at the meeting was a copy of *ECKANKAR—The Key to Secret Worlds*. It surprised her to see that its first publishing date had not been until 1969. Yet both the man and book looked exactly the same: just as she remembered them from the San Francisco hotel lobby in the mid-1950s. The lost memory of that initial meeting with the Master, a Spiritual Traveler, came rushing in like a flood in a desert.

The intervening years had given her time to

On the other hand, a greeting from the Master, the Godman, the Wayshower, may have a powerful impact, sparking a sharp reaction in the person.

finish the inner preparation needed to recognize him.

The trials of everyday living do indeed prepare one to meet the Master. They temper him to appreciate Soul Travel. Hardships and difficulties soon convince him of one thing: the Master can deliver Soul from spiritual darkness.

And so, Beth had found the Giver of God's Light and Sound.

After one's initial meeting with the Mahanta, the Master often uses the dream state to prepare an individual for receiving the divine Light and Sound of God.

The trials of everyday living do indeed prepare one to meet the Master.

The Blue Light of ECK

Tom calls New York City home and lives there with his family. He'd been feeling a real concern for the safety of his loved ones because of runaway street crime and the drug problem. Such things were commonplace in his neighborhood.

His mother, June, is a pious Catholic. She knew next to nothing about Eckankar and showed even less inclination to do so.

Of course, Tom worried about her safety as well as that of other relatives living in the area. So he talked to the inner side of the Master, the Mahanta. (We say "the Mahanta, the Living ECK Master," but other terms for him include the Inner Master or the Dream Master.) In his conversation with the Mahanta, Tom said, "If it's OK and I'm not interfering in my mother's space, is there some way to provide protection for her?"

About the same time he was talking with the Inner Master, June was praying at home. She'd felt a real dread of becoming a crime victim. So, in her prayer she pleaded, "God, please send me a guardian angel."

A short time later, as she sat in her living room, a beautiful blue light appeared.

ECKists refer to it as the Blue Light of the Mahanta. The Mahanta is the highest state of consciousness known to the chronicles of mankind, and this blue light often appears during contemplation. It tells of the presence of the Mahanta. The Blue Light makes no distinctions between religions. People in religions other than Eckankar sometimes speak of it, too, but without understanding its nature. However, they do sense that the Blue Light comes to render a blessing, give consolation to the heart, assurance to the spirit, and healing to the body.

The Blue Light of the Mahanta is, then, one of countless ways the Inner Master may show up and pass along the assurance of protection.

When June fell asleep that night—and remember, she knew next to nothing about Eckankar but its name—she had a dream. In it she felt a strong, unfamiliar urging. She later said, "I had to sing HU."

HU is a love song to God that ECKists like to sing. It's a very old name for God familiar to Muslims, primitive tribes, and others. The word helps open the heart, to spread its wings like a dove. "To open your wings" means to open your state of consciousness, like a blooming rose.

This is what June saw in her dream: a bright

The Blue Light of the Mahanta is one of countless ways the Inner Master may pass along the assurance of protection.

light wrapped itself around her, as light and airy as chiffon. It was the very same kind of Blue Light that had so startled her in the living room. Back then, when she'd told Tom of the light, he pointed to the spiritual tie-in between the Blue Light and the Inner Master, Wah Z. The dream lent June full assurance that God had indeed sent a guardian angel in answer to her prayer.

Her heart was free of worry and finally at peace.

Softly singing "Z" or "Wah Z" at bedtime will prepare you to meet me in your dreamlands.

About the Spiritual Names of ECK Masters

Z, or Wah Z, is my spiritual name; I answer to either.

The spiritual name of an ECK Master has a real, life-giving power. Whispering or softly singing "Z" or "Wah Z" at bedtime will prepare you to meet me in your dreamlands. Such meetings bring peace and rest. Some exciting adventures and revelations lie in store for you. ECK dreams are a spiritual way to lift you among the heavenly stars.

Some ECK Masters do have spiritual names that stand as both first and last names. Some people call Rebazar Tarzs "Rebazar" for short, but his full spiritual name is Rebazar Tarzs.

Lai Tsi's name is also two words; others always address him as Lai Tsi.

Other names are simpler, being only one word. A few that come to mind are Milarepa, Agnotti, Castrog, Gakko, Rama, and Malati. Learn more about these wonderful ECK Adepts in the booklet *ECK Wisdom Temples, Spiritual Cities, & Guides: A Brief History.*

The Upper Room

An ECKist who dances to the rhythm of life matures into an understanding of his relationship with the Mahanta, the Living ECK Master—especially with the Inner Master.

Susan is an ECKist who ran a catering service from her home. For a long time she'd fostered the notion that an upper room existed over her office, it being on a parallel inner plane. It was a haunting impression and always there. Yet where was the actual knowledge or experience to confirm this impression? There'd been none. But this feeling about the existence of such an upper room hung in the air every time she prepared food at home. It frightened her. She didn't know the reason for her ungrounded fear; nevertheless, it was always there.

One day in contemplation she decided the day had come to pierce the screen of mystery hiding the meaning of this unseen presence, which so troubled her peace of mind. What was it about that upper room? Why did it provoke such dread in her? Susan had to know. So she shut her eyes to meet the Inner Master in contemplation. And Wah Z, the Inner Master, did come to her. He wore white clothes and shoes.

"Come along," he said. "You want to go to the upper room?" She held back.

Kindly, the Master said, "Take my hand."

She shut her eyes to meet the Inner Master in contemplation. And Wah Z, the Inner Master, did come to her.

She took it, and he led the way up the steps
to the upper room. Her fear, however, tagged along,
sapping her courage. They approached the door;
Wah Z threw it wide open.

"Would you like to go in?"

He was offering to admit her to a higher state
of consciousness, but she didn't know what he
meant.

It was a king-size, spacious room, filled with
Light and Sound. This Light and Sound are of God
and together are the Voice of God, the Holy Spirit
of the sacred scriptures. The Holy Spirit appears
in this manner to those well along the spiritual
path. These, the fortunate few, may see the Light
as shades of blue, green, pink, or white, and in any
number of different forms. Sound, the other part
of God's Voice—indeed, the most important side
of it—may also speak in various ways. It could be
like a whistling teakettle, the pure notes of a flute
or violin, birdsongs, the wail of a far-away train
locomotive, or even bells.

These are actual sounds. People often tell of
hearing them in contemplation, a backdrop to the
hum of common everyday noise.

Wah Z, the Inner Master, repeated his invitation. "Here's the upper room. Would you care to
go in?" Susan stared openmouthed at the well-lit,
princely room beyond the door. A bright, but
magically soft light provided illumination for it.
Meanwhile, an all-encompassing and pleasant
music, a restful melody, soothed her troubled heart.

This heavenly Sound was the delightful Voice
of God; It was speaking directly to her. And as It

did, all was right within her worlds.

Then Wah Z said, "Let's go. We'll come back and do it all over again." And they did just that.

Over and over, Wah Z showed her the upper room. In so doing, he was saying, "Are you willing to go into this higher state of consciousness? Are you willing to make a commitment to go into this upper room?"

Susan had been afraid before. The human condition—that of the average person—is terrified of going outside itself. Wah Z, however, had granted her this Soul Travel journey. It changed her forever.

Such is the power of Soul Travel to uplift all people into a higher state of consciousness.

Susan had a revelation after her third return to this splendid room with Wah Z. Entering the room was actually the least important thing to her. More significant was her openhearted acceptance of her new, higher state of consciousness. But going into the room, of course, made her new spiritual state possible. Susan did overlook that life-giving connection at first. It came later, in a natural way.

Going into the room was therefore the most crucial part of the experience. From then on however, she was at complete ease whenever the Master led her to that upper room, her new state of consciousness.

Certainly in ECK we recognize many valid degrees of consciousness and experiences of other people. The higher and finer those states are, the more love and purity one may expect from the

Such is the power of Soul Travel to uplift all people into a higher state of consciousness.

individuals who have them. And the greater the purity, the more simple and honest are their hearts.

Susan learned all this via Soul Travel. She was now at peace and could enjoy her new freedom.

You and the Inner Teachings

The inner teachings will fit you like custom-made clothing of the finest material.

The inner teachings will fit you like custom-made clothing of the finest material. No outer teaching could ever do so. There are dozens of limitations upon the outer teachings, like the language of a chela (spiritual student) and his level of literacy.

I continue to sit down at my desk to write the ECK articles and letters to help you spiritually. Yet it is necessary to address you as part of a group consciousness. In other words, I have to determine the strongest pulse of the ECK audience to answer your spiritual needs. Then I speak to your heart, a one-on-one communication. At best, however, this approach can only address the general needs of any one individual.

Still, this approach is successful. It shows you how to reach the Inner Master, who can tailor the inner teachings to your spiritual needs.

The Inner Master welcomes you in the dream state and speaks to you like an old friend. He offers the spiritual help most appropriate that very hour. It certainly is a claim that no pastor, priest, or rabbi would dare to make. Help for the hour is truly one of the chief benefits of the inner teachings of ECK. My talks and writings tell story upon story of people who've met the ECK Masters in their dreams and so discovered a gold mine rich with countless nuggets of true value.

Belief in the Master's ever-present company relies upon an individual's degree of unfoldment. Actual inner experiences help one move to a greater understanding of the ways of divine revelation. But if he chooses to hang on to shopworn karmic debts due to, say, an inability to control some mental passion or habit like anger, then his spiritual momentum stops. It's that simple. Of course, a headstrong follower always tries to fix blame on the Mahanta, the Living ECK Master when his attempts to advance in ECK come to nothing.

But such an attitude changes nothing. The individual is a loser and will continue to be a loser until he adopts the practices of a winner.

I'm used to such misdirected slings. They go with my position. I realize that at some point an individual will break free of his holding pattern and again soar higher. It's when he's seen that all responsibility for his unfoldment lies with him alone.

Actual inner experiences help one move to a greater understanding of the ways of divine revelation.

Lesson on a Mountain

Tim knew full well of a troubling, deep-seated anger holding him back in life. It stole all joy and peace of mind. This anger reaped a harvest of unwanted misery. Then, an inner change brought him face-to-face with truth; fortunately, he knew to turn to the Inner Master.

One day during a spiritual exercise, Tim found himself sitting on a mountainside with Wah Z, the

Mahanta. It was the ideal occasion to pose a spiritual question. Maybe the Master's answer could unravel the awful knot of anger that ruled his life.

"Why do I react to this earth world with such anger?" he asked.

In response, Wah Z pointed over the crag on which they'd stopped to rest their feet. Tim looked over the side and gaped; his disordered mind began to spin. The dizzying height struck him with vertigo, and he quickly backed clear of the crag's edge.

Wah Z spoke a single word: "Fear."

The word prompted an immediate insight for Tim. He realized he'd provided a home for fear, reluctance to let go and leap into the abyss of life, because he failed to trust God's love for him.

Wah Z told Tim about St. Francis of Assisi, someone who'd once chanced a blind leap of faith. To paint a picture for emphasis, the Master took him back along the Time Track to the eleventh century, to the place St. Francis had established his monastery. But Wah Z voiced a word of caution to him. There was no advantage for Tim or anyone else who desired a spiritual healing to ever become an ascetic.

The point, Wah Z said, was that St. Francis was never one to let unhappiness steal his heart from God.

A radiating white light from somewhere above them caught Tim's attention. It brought complete peace, offering a therapeutic serenity Tim hadn't felt in a long, long time. In its wake came instruc-

"Why do I react to this earth world with such anger?" he asked. Wah Z spoke a single word: "Fear."

tions from Wah Z to release all emotional ties with people he'd ever had a romantic relationship with in this lifetime.

So Tim embarked upon a campaign of spiritual cleansing. Only then did he recognize the terrible grip those memories and attachments had on him. Each one that Tim released into the white light of ECK brought him more freedom and happiness.

That is the way of a spiritual healing.

The True Test of a Master

You are Soul. It is the real you. You aren't the outerwear of human material that the unenlightened think is the real them. And Soul is the you that I can and wish to help.

One way the Inner Master comes is when you see the Divine Light. On the other hand, you could first hear the Sound of God, which may come as the single, reedy note of a flute. Perhaps you'll catch the chirping of crickets, in a season when there are no crickets around. The Holy Sound Current could also come to you like a deep humming, or like atoms rushing about in some microworld. These Sounds of God, and others, are really the play of atoms on some higher spiritual plane. The many Sounds are a guidepost to your present state of consciousness. Any divine Sound you hear in contemplation or dreams gives the assurance of a spiritual renewal.

The path of ECK also hastens a wrapping up of karmic patterns. Life becomes nothing less than

You are Soul. It is the real you. And Soul is the you I can and wish to help.

a bold and fruitful adventure.

Of course, there's no guarantee in ECK that a burning off of karma will deliver a life of ease, prosperity, or happiness. But it will bring spiritual freedom. And as you advance in that direction, you will notice a change for the better in your thoughts and feelings.

You'll learn to cooperate with the unerring will of the Holy Spirit. You learn how to let things be. In ECK, we offer up the ancient benediction of the Vairagi Adepts: "May the blessings be." It gives a choice of whether to accept or turn aside the blessing. It will not impose itself.

All have a right to noninterference.

I come in your dreams as the Mahanta, the Inner Master. And what is a reliable test of any Master? Does he carry a God-given power to spiritually lift you into the higher worlds?

That is the test.

You have only to seek the Mahanta, today's Living ECK Master. He is God's elect. He's given his life over to help you find God's love and compassion, to speed your journey home.

The road to God-Realization may be difficult but there is help available.

Who Is Sri Harold Klemp?

The road to God-Realization may be difficult and seemingly impassable at times, but there is help available for one who desires God above all else.

My first awareness of such assistance came during my senior year in high school at a Lutheran college, which prepared high-school and college students for later seminary study, to become ministers. This college offered a superb liberal-arts program.

Yet my doubts about becoming a minister had grown with each passing year of high school.

Five years earlier, at thirteen, while still an immature eighth grader, I had decided to become a minister. Certainly no one forced this decision upon me, but once made, it was not easy to undo.

The campus was in Milwaukee, Wisconsin's largest city. Soon after my arrival there, a haunting thought came to mind: would this place actually become my prison? It was a good city, but my heart ached for the kind of freedom I'd enjoyed on the farm. But after all their sacrifices to pay the tuition and board, my parents would not hear of my leaving school in the first year. They felt I should give it a chance. So one year slipped to another until I was suddenly a senior. My decision about whether to become a minister was as uncertain as it had ever been.

That's when I met a remarkable stranger. He seemed to appear from nowhere.

One pleasant spring day, I took a long walk to reflect on this matter. And that's when I met a remarkable stranger. He seemed to appear from nowhere.

Our meeting began with a mutual agreement about the beauty and grace of the botanical garden that lay off to one side of the walk. Soon he had me telling of my uncertainty about the future. A few probing questions later he had me wrestling with profound concepts about salvation.

The stranger discoursed on God's profound

love for mankind. He also made a prediction. He said I would indeed find the assurance of salvation I was seeking, but it would come from a quarter outside of my religion. You can imagine that I had no idea what he was talking about. Outside the Lutheran Church? I couldn't conceive of such a thing.

Years later, however, I would speculate about whether this fellow was one of those unknown ECK Masters I had since learned of.

I did follow his advice to pursue my education through college. Many of my most searching questions about religious doctrine needed more time to reach maturity before I would be ready to understand and accept the answers.

One night, three years later, a terrifying event occurred that raised a whole new set of concerns.

Sleep had refused to come. So I lay on my bunk, eyes fixed above me. Then a most startling thing happened. My Spiritual Eye, as I determined a few years later, had somehow opened. Above me was a most incredible sight: beautiful white fluffy clouds floated upon a sea of sparkling blue. The clouds parted; a fortress appeared. This fortress was of the old style, a remnant of the hoary, biblical days of Jericho. Its walls, too high to scale, were not of rubies, diamonds, or other precious gems as might be hoped for in a fortress that otherwise gave every appearance of being a celestial wonder. They were built instead of sturdy, gigantic blocks of stone. In front of me there rose two mighty gates, the only visible entrance into this bastion of ages past.

One night three years later a most startling thing happened.

Then, a voice spoke from nowhere and every-where at once. Years later I would recognize it as the unmistakable voice of Paul Twitchell, founder of modern-day Eckankar.

It was a man's soft voice, tinged with a South-ern accent. It said, "You will see and know what no man has ever seen and known before." My mind tripped over itself in a blind panic. "If this knowledge is so great and special," my mind whis-pered, "might it not also kill you?"

Frantic with fear, I screamed in that world with all my being, "No! I don't want to see and know *anything!*" The vision began to melt into the void of its origin.

I found myself alone, seated on my bed in absolute confusion. I shivered, soaked through and through with sweat.

Dear God, what was that?

What was that?

In the morning, with only snatches of tor-mented sleep, I sought the solace of a little one-man chapel in the basement of our dorm. I prayed for, begged for, comfort and guidance from Christ.

Then, something happened again. I awoke in what I would later know to be the Soul body. I hovered high above the earth. I was floating in space like a pair of all-seeing eyes. Then I became conscious of a sort of umbilical cord trailing be-hind me. Whatever was it for? It came along into the outer reaches of space, a somehow comforting thing to have along for a companion. It seemed that the silvery, pulsing thing was a lifeline of some kind; it fed my religious faith.

A man's voice said, "You will see and know what no man has ever seen and known before."

Trouble!

I saw that someone had dared to cut it in two with golden scissors. The severed cord vanished, drifting away, swallowed by the black oblivion of space.

I then slipped back into my physical self.

The vision had flown. I was left alone to survey my shattered confidence in years of biblical training. Things like this experience just were not supposed to happen. Yet they had. And I now suspected that a key element was missing from the heart of my religious education.

This vision was to be another step toward Eckankar, still some five years in my future.

Next, my sheltered school days with an occupational deferment lost out to a tour of duty in the air force. In 1967, then, I found the Eckankar teachings while at Yokota Air Base, Japan, when I replied to a small ad by Paul Twitchell in *Fate* magazine. My unfoldment was about to shift into high gear.

My unfoldment was about to shift into high gear.

And it surely did.

Fourteen years later, in 1981, I was to accept the role of spiritual leader of Eckankar and serve as the Mahanta, the Living ECK Master. In my book *Autobiography of a Modern Prophet,* the story of the extensive inner and outer training that preceded this occasion is set down in greater detail. It describes my encounter with the experience of God-Realization in the spring of 1970.

It was on October 22, 1981, that I received the Rod of ECK Power, which is the power of the Word of God entrusted to the one chosen by the

Sugmad (God) to handle the awesome responsibility of helping others gain spiritual freedom.
And so the spiritual energy of the Rod of ECK
Power transfers from the Living ECK Master to
his successor. And with the Rod of ECK Power
comes the all-seeing and all-knowing vision of the
Mahanta Consciousness. The new Living ECK
Master, upon accepting his mission, wins recognition in the Order of Vairagi Adepts, who ac-
knowledge him as the main vehicle for the
primordial Mahanta.

What was my mission to be?

What was my mission to be? ECK Master Fubbi Quantz revealed the task to me.

The Mission Foretold

Years earlier, in November 1978, the ECK-
Vidya, ancient science of prophecy, had forecast a
major shift in direction for Eckankar during my
cycle as the Mahanta, the Living ECK Master. ECK
Master Fubbi Quantz revealed the task to me.
He'd opened a window to the future and pointed
to a water channel (the ECK teachings) that needed
a brisk scrubbing. While cleaning it, I noticed how
the entire channel was subdivided into scores of
well-defined units. Each unit encompassed a certain time frame. And each represented the mission objective of a certain Living ECK Master from
the past or future.

The water channel was like a plumbing pipe
with a number of joints or elbow joints. The channel made a right-angled turn in my section.

Fubbi Quantz said that during my term of
office, the teachings of ECK would need a

revamping, to present them in a fresh, new way. I was to introduce the high teachings of ECK into the everyday lives of people.

So I took great care to clean and scrub my section of the channel until it sparkled like polished silver.

This prophecy is turning out as Fubbi Quantz had foreseen. The presentation of the ECK teachings in common, everyday terms makes them easy to understand by all who are ready to receive them.

My section of the channel had linked two different directions in Eckankar. The previous section used an approach with a strong appeal for metaphysicians, who love the intellectual side of such teachings. So that approach is already covered in the ECK teachings. But now comes an approach that meets the needs of people who must shop, put food on the table, and also find family time. Both approaches, however, remind ECK initiates to always be aware of this very moment. Why rush the natural tempo and order of your spiritual progress?

Everyone is in his rightful place, at this and every moment.

Every Master knows full well that the thrust of the teachings must address the consciousness of people today, because today's lessons are the most important of all. They help us build for tomorrow.

Every individual, then, gets from the ECK teachings exactly what he puts into them.

Everyone is in his rightful place, at this and every moment.

Three Bodies of the Mahanta

Sometimes a student of ECK catches a profound insight into the workings of Sugmad's plan. Kira was one who had such good fortune.

She was at an ECK seminar where I was to speak by satellite. She waited for the telecast to start. Kira joined the audience in singing the HU song.

With her eyes still shut, she saw the Master, but he was only visible from the waist up. Over his head appeared a thin shaft of white light. A more youthful image of the Master slowly descended this shaft of light until his image entered the top of his physical being. Seconds later a bright white light began to radiate from his eyes. The light became more intense; it streamed from his face, enveloping it in a magnificent brilliance.

The Mahanta Consciousness, she realized, is an inseparable part of the Master.

His face was nothing less than a lantern of pure white light.

At this, Kira opened her eyes, expecting to see the Master's telecast image on the projection screen, but the telecast hadn't begun.

Kira pondered this experience for days. Had she seen the Mahanta Consciousness enter the Master before he began his talk? She didn't know. But it happened that one of the Mahanta Transcripts books held the answer. The Mahanta Consciousness, she realized, is an inseparable part of the Master.

So what was the full scope of what she'd seen?

The Shariyat-Ki-Sugmad speaks of the three aspects of the Sugmad (God). First is the primordial, the eternal Mahanta. This is the clear Voice of God. It dwells in the heart of the Ocean of Love and Mercy. Second is the body of glory. This is the ECK, the Cosmic Spirit, the Sound Current. It is the breath of life behind creation, all life, giving sustenance to all things seen and unseen, known and yet to know.

Third is the historical Mahanta, the Living ECK Master. He is the Eternal One, the bodily manifestation of Sugmad.

Kira had witnessed the channel of the primordial Mahanta opening wide. In her experience, it was the "younger version" of the Master. Her insight was certainly a gift from the ECK, for it brought upliftment, purification, and understanding.

What Is the Mahanta?

Maria said, "Sing HU. It's an ancient name for God; you can sing it for help in times of trouble."

Maria has enjoyed a close, loving relationship with the Mahanta over the years, even before this lifetime. It is her experience that there is ever more divine love to discover.

One day Maria set out on a walk, making her way along city streets for a chiropractic adjustment. Near the courthouse, a young woman approached her. Could Maria spare a moment?

"What is it?" Maria asked.

"Give me words of wisdom!"

It was clearly an unusual request. Maria studied the woman as she gathered her thoughts. Then she said, "Sing HU."

Maria showed her the way to do it, explaining, "It's an ancient name for God; you can sing it for help in times of trouble or when you're feeling down." The young woman's eyes filled with tears, and they began spilling down her cheeks. She held out her arm for a handshake before she left. Then each went her separate way, but both were deeply moved by the power of their chance meeting.

The rest of the day, Maria's thoughts kept returning to that meeting. Then a sudden thought came to the fore.

Earlier that day she'd asked the ECK, What is the Mahanta? Oh, she knew, of course, but her heart burned ardently for an even greater knowledge of that magnificent power. Sometimes she'll sense the Mahanta's presence; at other times she'll have a clear and radiant dream. Maria had felt prepared for an even greater realization of his closeness to her. Now she recognized this experience with the woman near the courthouse as the Mahanta's direct reply to her request.

Earlier that day she'd asked the ECK, What is the Mahanta?

The Holy Spirit does truly answer every prayer of the heart. Maria thus received satisfaction for her question. The Mahanta, the Living ECK Master, she knows, is the all-seeing, all-knowing, love of God.

When the Time Is Right

To review: we find two sides to the ECK teachings—the inner and the outer. The outer teachings come from the outer person—the Living ECK Master. As such, he writes discourses, articles, and gives talks. On the inner side—the greater side— the Mahanta appears as counterpart to the Living

ECK Master, helping people in the dream state. Here the Mahanta is also known as the Dream Master.

The Inner Master and the Outer Master are, of course, one and the same: the Mahanta, the Living ECK Master. It is important to understand that the Master is one being.

The Outer Master provides the books and teachings of ECK to acquaint you with the elements of the whats, wheres, and whys of the boundless inner worlds. He does this to inform you of the endless possibilities of unfoldment on the inner planes.

People who stick with their spiritual exercises and go into contemplation, discover the eternal Dream Master, simply a manifestation of the divine ECK. He provides them with food from God's own table, which supplies their every spiritual need.

Grace and the Dream Master

Grace came into this life destined to meet the Dream Master, to receive his support in her quest for God Consciousness. At eighteen, growing up in Nigeria, she suffered the anguish of emotional and psychic miseries; it made life a nightmare. Now and again, she wished to leave this earth forever.

Then Grace, who'd not ever heard of Eckankar, had a life-changing dream with the Dream Master.

Her dream guide lifted her from a deep slum-

ber and said, "Pay attention!" He began to introduce her to new and exciting ideas, by tracing on
her bedroom wall the course of her spiritual journey for ages yet to come.

Grace recognized him. He was an old and
trusted friend, teacher, and spiritual guide. What
a joy to see him! It seemed she had waited for him
far too long, for ages. Yet a sixth sense had urged
her to be patient, because somewhere in her heart
she *knew* he would come at the most opportune
time.

Grace sought to capture for her waking
memory what he was writing on the wall. But he
wrote far too fast for her to read or copy his notes.
And his hand! It was pure gold from wrist to
fingertips. Grace asked him to write slower.

He replied, "All you need is to pay attention."
She would recall everything needed in a critical
hour.

So she left off fretting.

Grace awoke back in her bed and recorded the
few things still lodged in memory after her futile
attempt to keep pace with the Dream Master.
She recalled two words the guide had written in
bold letters across the wall, highlighted in large
blue letters and outlined in gold. She jotted down
the words *Eckankar* and *Wah Z*, with the spellings
only a little jumbled. Yet it was the best she could
do.

Within two years, she would find the teachings of ECK, courtesy of a friend. To be more
accurate, they sought her out. Circumstances the
following year turned up a picture of the Master.

*The Dream
Master began
to introduce
her to new and
exciting ideas,
by tracing on
her bedroom
wall the course
of her spiritual
journey for
ages yet to
come.*

Still, it wasn't until the Inner Master had given her a nudge to review her dream journal that she finally made the connection: this Wah Z was her dream guide. It'd taken her twenty years to come to this point. But now she felt assured that her newfound link with the Mahanta was all she would ever need.

Today she knows that Soul is her true self. She is a timeless, deathless spark of God—in love, strength, and beauty—upheld by the always present Light and Sound, the Holy Spirit.

Today she knows that Soul is her true self. She is a timeless, deathless spark of God upheld by the always present Light and Sound, the Holy Spirit.

A Promise Kept

Eileen first discovered Eckankar in 1967. She'd studied two years under Paul Twitchell but then left the path without taking the Second Initiation in ECK, which he had offered to her. She was afraid of making such a commitment to ECK. Five years later, with many more bruisings from life's trials behind her, she stood looking out her bedroom window. Eileen wept bitterly. She'd lost spiritually by leaving the path of ECK back then. Paul Twitchell, for example, had translated (died) a year before.

Yet that same night Eileen awoke in the dream state.

She was walking along a country road where tall cornstalks rose like sentinels on either side. Up ahead a colorful field splashed with bright blue flowers awaited her. A white picket fence surrounded them. There, too, was a man in a blue suit.

Oh, what was his name?

Well, it didn't matter, because she knew he was the Living ECK Master. She ran to him. The Master simply opened his arms then held her, while Eileen cried with joy and gratitude. In a moment, she looked around. Three white monuments poked up among the flowers; this field was a graveyard.

"Who is buried here, Master?" she asked. The names on the stones were hard to read.

"These stones represent three Souls who will translate (pass on) from earth," he said. "When the third Soul translates (dies), you will return to me."

Five years later, her only son died; three more years, her father; and seven years after that, her mother-in-law. The day following her mother-in-law's death, Eileen's husband asked her to meet a woman who'd come to console them. Although the woman and her husband were customers of the family business, Eileen had never met them. The woman introduced herself as a member of the clergy. "My name is Marcia," she said. "I am an ECKist." Eileen, surprised, said she was too. Despite many long years of not being a member of Eckankar, Eileen still thought of herself as a member of ECK.

Marcia presented Eileen with an ECK video-cassette, which provided the answer to an old and haunting mystery: the name of the man in her dream. In a letter to me she wrote, "It was then I learned the man who had held me in a field of blue flowers fifteen years before was you, Harold. Thank you!"

An ECK videocassette provided the answer to an old and haunting mystery: the name of the man in her dream.

All answers come at the right time and in the right place, as they did for Eileen.

Your Freedom Is My Reward

The mission of the Mahanta, the Living ECK Master is unlike those of the saviors sent by the Kal (the negative power), who come to improve social and political conditions.

The Mahanta, the Living ECK Master comes simply to free Souls from karma and reincarnation. He offers the Spiritual Exercises of ECK to accomplish that.

The Mahanta, the Living ECK Master comes simply to free Souls from karma and reincarnation. He offers the Spiritual Exercises of ECK to accomplish that, and it is he alone who carries the Rod of ECK Power. It lets him lift into the heavenly kingdom all who truly seek it. He restores Soul to the heaven of heavens, to Its real home, the Ocean of Love and Mercy.

So the Mahanta, the Living ECK Master offers deliverance from this world instead of improved social or living conditions within it.

Such is the Mahanta's unconditional love for Soul. Soul's attraction to the Master is the most natural bond in the world, because both the Master and his disciple (chela) desire the very same thing: spiritual liberation. He provides the one and only way for It to receive the full measure of God's love, and do it in this selfsame incarnation.

And what are the Spiritual Exercises of ECK? They connect your everyday, human consciousness with your divine calling. They help clear the way, so you may sooner recognize the Voice of God as It gently guides you through the uncertainties and trials of everyday living.

And you will learn to hear It speak.

Ears to Hear

Lisa often has special conversations with the Inner Master. When life presses too hard, like a fist in the back, she turns to him for love and guidance.

On one occasion, she wanted assurance that her relationship with the Mahanta was secure, or had the ebb and flow of self-doubt tangled their tender love bond? She wanted to know. So she went into contemplation to talk this matter over with him.

The next day Lisa's ears began to trill with an exquisite, shimmering sound. It was much louder than she is used to hearing the Sound Current.

"Thank you, Mahanta!" she whispered.

To her surprise and delight, she heard the Master's crystal-clear voice say, "So did you think I've been speaking to you in English?"

No, not in English. He usually addressed her through the pure Voice of God. And this same inner side of the Master is always with you. Some say, "I call the Master, and then he comes." That's not exactly the case, since the Master is always present.

So be assured that I am always with you.

When a chela (spiritual student) sings HU to open his heart, he comes to recognize the ever-abiding grace and presence of the Mahanta, who really is with him by the moment. He is *always* with him, because the Mahanta is the Spirit of God Itself.

Lisa was now content; her heart was still. The love of the Master was indeed with her, to ease life's pressures.

To her surprise and delight, she heard the Master's crystal-clear voice say, "So did you think I've been speaking to you in English?"

The Master's Touch

Amy was reflecting upon a passage in *The Shariyat-Ki-Sugmad*, scriptures of ECK. She was curious about the physical presence of the Mahanta, the Living ECK Master. The passage in question spoke of blessings being passed from Sugmad (God) through the Mahanta, then on to a chela. The Master does it by shaking hands, giving a kiss, or gently touching a chela with the tip of his finger.

Amy searched her memory. She'd witnessed his meetings with ECK initiates many times and had often observed the Darshan, when a disciple meets the Master, who recognizes him. Yet for all those many occasions, she'd never, ever seen the Master touch someone with his fingertip. Why did *The Shariyat* specifically say "tip of his finger"? How odd it was that of the many times she'd read this passage, she never noticed the reference about the fingertip. True, *The Sharyiat* did often speak in a poetic fashion, yet real truth lay behind every word and reference.

Why did The Shariyat *specifically say "tip of his finger"?*

So Amy took her bewilderment on this point to the Mahanta in contemplation.

Later that same day, the Mahanta, the Living ECK Master met with the Eckankar staff; he greeted old and dear friends. There were smiles, hugs, and handshakes all around. And with this display of affection between the Master and his beloved aides, Amy began to hear the heavenly Sound Current. It was pouring through the ethers. She watched and felt the purification and blessings of the Holy Spirit fill all whom the Master met.

And then something caught Amy's eye. After he'd warmly hugged a long-standing friend and ECK initiate, he drew back. And as he did so, he gently caressed a stray hair of the individual into place.

With his fingertip!

This sign of tender affection might be of no consequence in some people's books, but Amy watched in awe as the Master's spiritual demonstration played out before her. The Sound Current was now so very strong. She'd witnessed the heart of *The Shariyat*, the Darshan of the Master, and the miracle of the Mahanta's blessing in that one simple gesture. The love of the Mahanta overlooks no detail. He fulfills a chela's desire to learn the hidden ways of ECK. He knows all things; he is a servant of life itself.

The Inner Master is not a physical being, but the matrix of the eternal Life Force that appears to you on the inner planes in contemplation or the dream state. He may look like me, like another ECK Master, or even like Christ.

All his inner form really is, however, is the merging of the Light and Sound of God into a matrix that appears in a guise that an ordinary person can relate to and approach.

The Master, then, is the inner guide. He steers his charges around the pits of karma, the troubles they've made for themselves due to an inborn resistance to the spiritual laws of life. His image is a focal point through which the Holy Spirit descends, then ascends, lifting each and every purified Soul into a higher plane, there to bathe

She'd witnessed the heart of The Shariyat, *the Darshan of the Master, and the miracle of the Mahanta's blessing in that one simple gesture.*

in the splendid love of the One Supreme God.

Think of the Mahanta as the personalized ECK. He is a transformer. He steps down the full might of the God Stream and regulates Its flow to accommodate the unique vibrations of every Soul.

That is one of his many functions.

He is thus the Divine Essence that appears in a far-reaching form that people can understand. Speaking in a broad yet accurate sense, the ECK and the Mahanta are one.

Paid in Full

Sometimes people don't understand the role of a spiritual guide, whether it's the Mahanta, Christ, Buddha, or another religious figure. All of them have a special connection of some kind with the Holy Spirit. A true spiritual master is an instrument for the Voice of God. He appears in human form to serve people in a way they can understand, to reveal to them the workings of Divine Spirit in everyday life.

The Mahanta, the Living ECK Master has the ability and authority to alter an individual's fate.

In Eckankar, then, this divine force declares Itself through the Outer and Inner Master. He can thus assist and teach Souls here and in the invisible worlds.

The Mahanta, the Living ECK Master also has the ability and authority to alter an individual's fate. This, of course, is a remarkable benefit. The Master will adjust the individual's destiny at certain levels of spiritual unfoldment. In this way, excess karma can be burned off in the dream state.

So do your spiritual exercises. Avoid many unpleasant karmic repayments. And soon, your Book of Records will see the Master's notation: "Paid in full."

*   *   *

The Mahanta, the Living ECK Master also helps in other ways. An unusual example of a spiritual healing follows:

Kate had an unusual problem. Whenever she shopped for food, she had to brace herself for the produce department, due to a strong aversion to dinosaur kale, of all things. She called it "dino kale." It is a hardy green vegetable in the cabbage family but of a much darker green. Its leaves are dappled with nubby bumps. For some strange reason, Kate had a fearful dread of this harmless green garden plant. The mere sight of it brought on awful feelings of panic and repulsion.

Kate had an unusual problem. The mere sight of this harmless garden plant brought on feelings of panic.

She avoided looking it in the eye, so to speak.

One day, early in the couple's marriage, her husband arrived home from the health food store and began to fill the refrigerator with fresh foods he'd just bought. Kate threw an uneasy glance at an inoffensive-looking paper bag on the kitchen counter. An inner signal sent a warning.

Kale?

"What's that?" she asked.

Her husband reached for the bag to look. Kate drew back from the counter, hands in front of her eyes, with pounding heart. Panic swept her. Tears threatened as the opened bag did indeed reveal the dreaded dino kale. Her husband saw her unnatural reaction and quickly removed the offensive bag from the house and threw it in the trash. He returned to comfort Kate, but what could he say?

Kate was usually practical to the nth degree. Moreover, she also had the curiosity of a scientist. Why such a reaction toward dino kale? She had to find out.

So she took the matter into contemplation, to ask the Mahanta to please enlighten her.

He showed her a link to a past life. He said that the source of her fear was from a betrayal she'd once suffered from a race of people of another planet. Their skins resembled dino kale.

Kate was satisfied to learn the reason for her extreme fear, though it did not relieve it.

One day Kate was delivering a package to the Master's house. Joan, his wife, brought her into the kitchen, where the Master stood at the kitchen sink. He was preparing dinner. She watched him with fascination. He cut leaves of dino kale from their stems with great care. Dino kale! For some reason Kate felt perfectly safe in the Master's presence.

There wasn't even a trace of fear.

The Master had not just been cutting leaves from the stems of kale. In fact, he'd been cutting away that old karma responsible for her fear and panic.

Kate learned, too, that from that day on, she had no further qualms about dino kale. In fact, she now eats it with some regularity.

She knew the Master had not just been cutting leaves from the stems of kale. In fact, he'd been cutting away that old karma responsible for her fear and panic. Kate was grateful for the precious gift of love and freedom he'd given her.

Joy Asks to Finish Her Education

I always return to the definition of the Mahanta, the Living ECK Master as a Wayshower. He is not a way-pusher or a way-dragger, one who kicks or shoves you through the inner worlds.

The Wayshower is, quite simply, the one who shows you the way to your true home in the heart of God. He can show *you* the way home. He will accompany you through the inner worlds, pointing out where it's safe and warning where it's not. He is a Wayshower only for those who accept him. They must, however, carefully follow his instructions about the best way to go. The Master only wants to help you finish your spiritual education.

Now let's see how this works out in Joy's case.

Joy was a flight attendant for Austrian Airlines. One night the Mahanta appeared to her in a dream.

They were relaxing on a couch before a camera, as if in a broadcast studio to do a TV talk show. Joy played the part of an interviewer. She and the Master chatted casually over a cup of tea, the Master clarifying a few spiritual matters that'd troubled her. The atmosphere in the studio was like a day in spring, but soon she turned the discussion to an issue of real concern to her. Joy asked him about the length of his service as the Living ECK Master. How long would he serve in that position? Were there others in training?

The Master assured her that a few initiates were indeed training for leadership in ECK, but no one was ready yet to assume the responsibility. It might take several years or many more for the

The Wayshower will accompany you through the inner worlds, pointing out where it's safe and warning where it's not.

first one to complete all the tests. Accordingly, the Master would continue for another cycle as the Mahanta, the Living ECK Master.

Joy considered that. It seemed to her that far too many ECKists believed that the surest way to spiritual greatness was to sit at the Master's knee at ECK seminars. All that was necessary, they imagined, was to sop up his wisdom. Now she recognized that everyone had to get out there and do it. They had to engage in life. That's where the spiritual lessons were. All in ECK had to develop into well-rounded spiritual beings.

Joy recognized everyone had to engage in life. That's where the spiritual lessons were.

Even the small circle of candidates for the ECK Mastership had to earn their golden spurs.

*   *   *

Joy's dream later dovetailed with an experience on the physical plane.

Joy had gone to a movie with her boyfriend. The film portrayed the deeply felt emotions of the leading characters. They were locked fast in heavy iron chains of karma. While walking to the car after the show, Joy was lost in thought. Would she ever see the day where she'd get the upper hand on the five Soul-numbing passions of lust, anger, greed, vanity, and undue attachment?

And what were her chances of becoming an ECK Master?

Ah, the questions.

In silence she asked, "Will you, Mahanta, finish my education?" In that very moment, a huge fluorescent sign ahead flashed a welcome message to her. It read: "That can be arranged!"

Joy laughed with delight. So she really did live in the bosom of Sugmad. From that day on, she's had total confidence in the Master's everlasting love and guidance. It is the keystone of her spiritual life.

*   *   *

In this way Joy found a renewed energy behind her spiritual disciplines. Above all, she was learning how to be a channel for ECK (Cosmic Spirit).

Before a later contemplation she asked the Mahanta, "How is it possible to survive here?" Then she sang HU a couple of times, relaxed in silence, and watched the blank screen of her mind.

She asked the Mahanta, "How is it possible to survive here?"

Suddenly she became aware of being on another plane, where she'd often met Wah Z in the past. She followed a familiar wide path. White pebbles covered its surface as it curved along in a beautiful setting. From past experience Joy knew that Wah Z would be waiting for her around the next bend, sitting in the grass under a tree or leaning against the tree. He might also be on a bench, with the warm smile of a dear and treasured friend lighting his face.

And there he was! The Master emerged from the shadows of the trees with a broad smile the moment Joy rounded the bend. After a hug of greeting, Joy was curious. What now?

The Master led her along the winding path until they came to a fork. The left one gleamed with white pebbles; the right one had pebbles of a dull grey. The air in the direction of the right path was heavy and oppressive. Just looking along that fork made Joy uneasy. Joy was sure they'd go left. Instead, Wah Z chose the right fork and ignored her desire to take what looked to be the better route.

Soon they gained the crest of a mountain range that overlooked a grand, sweeping plain. Before her eyes there stretched a vast city with skyscrapers, houses, and industrial buildings on a desert of concrete. A red and grey mist attired the land like a thick and suffocating shroud. The place looked frightening, threatening, and even dangerous. Joy knew she was looking at home sweet home, the dear old physical plane.

She turned to the Master. "How is it possible to survive down there?"

A split second later she stood in the midst of the foreboding scene, the dull mist drifting in on all sides, like poison gas. The pervasive negativity was about to overcome her. How could she escape this terrible place?

But then the mercy of God caused a wonderful thing to happen.

Joy began to hear the sweet sound of HU. A steady ray of glittering light beamed a shield of protection from above.

Joy began to hear the sweet sound of HU. A steady ray of glittering light beamed a shield of protection from above and grew in magnificence and magnitude, its ray slicing through the dull fog. The HU became a roar of thunder. Together, the Light and Sound of God proved to be an invincible shield. The negative power vanished, leaving no trace behind.

Joy felt a breath of spiritual liberation riding the celestial winds.

Now Joy knew exactly how an individual can survive under any and all conditions: he must become an unobstructed channel for the mighty power of the ECK, be a vehicle for the Light and Sound of God. She gazed upon the changing scenery and watched the dull grey concrete transformed into living, beautiful shining green grass.

The holy light continued to reach out, touching everything and everybody in the whole world.

A Soul in pursuit of spiritual revelation may not ever shirk Its responsibilities. Who should care most whether you practice the spiritual exercises that the Master entrusts to you? You know the answer.

The answer is in your hands.

You've earned the right to them, so use them. Don't let mediocrity suffocate you in the thick red-and-grey fog of unknowing. The Spiritual Exercises of ECK are the lost passkey to life. They give the secrets of the ancient ones. Why be life's victim? A greater state of consciousness is a direct result of doing your spiritual exercises and will reveal new ways to ease your life.

Such freedom is but one of the many benefits that come to all who wish to find the living way and do something about it.

Some of my teachings are simply instructions on how to do a certain thing. They come complete with guidelines. My purpose is this: to awaken the knowledge and love for the divine things that now lie sleeping in your heart.

You are Soul, a child of God. It is your good fortune to eventually become a Co-worker with

The Spiritual Exercises of ECK are the lost passkey to life. They give the secrets of the ancient ones.

God. The way of ECK is the single, most important choice you can ever make. Your spiritual freedom is my reward.

I am always with you.

A Spiritual Exercise to Meet the Mahanta

In contemplation or before sleep, see yourself strolling on a beach. Sing *Harji, Wah Z,* or simply *Z.*

The Inner Master is always looking for his beloved follower to come in the Soul form.

Ahead of you on the sand is a blanket laden with fruit. The Inner Master, the Mahanta, awaits you there. He is always looking for his beloved follower to come in the Soul form. In his hands he cradles a goblet made of precious jewels. He offers it to you.

"In it is the water of life," he says. "Take it and drink."

The water of life is in fact the ECK, the Light and Sound of God. Drink all of It. Visualize the Light and Sound acting gently upon you. Once you drink of this cup, you will never again thirst for a lesser drink. You will always want these pure waters of heaven.

12
Your Spiritual
Destiny
A Star of God

*S*ome people spend their whole lives looking for ECK. And after many trials and false leads, they finally realize that elusive dream. It is a delightful day when they find ECK.

An openhearted truth seeker realizes that something inside is nudging him from the nest of his old beliefs. He rightly senses that the answers he is looking for do assuredly exist. This inner force pushing him toward that end is an urge beyond his conscious command.

This compulsion is the call of Soul.

Earth is exactly like a schoolroom. It's to provide each Soul, like you, with all the many experiences It needs to unfold spiritually: first, into becoming a Co-worker with the Mahanta, and then, a Co-worker with God.

These two areas of development and service are a natural part of the evolutionary cycles of Soul. The divine process of purification shapes our destiny once we let the Voice of God come into our heart with gladness and no misgivings.

An open-hearted truth seeker realizes that something inside is nudging him from the nest of his old beliefs.

Haunted by a Near-Death Experience

Lenny was one such seeker.

Some twenty years earlier, Lenny had gone hunting in a neighbor's field with his father, brother, and a neighbor friend. Tragedy was to change Lenny's life. Lightning struck both him and his neighbor, who died immediately. Lenny himself went into cardiac arrest. But his brother revived him en route to the hospital; in the emergency room, however, Lenny's heart then failed again.

The medical staff tried everything in its power to revive him, but without success. Grave, hopeless seconds flew away like falcons upon the wind. Unable to make out a sign of life, the doctor signaled a nurse to pull the plug. As she bent over to disconnect the monitors, the faintest bleep sounded from the EKG.

Life!

The team sprang into action reviving Lenny.

He lay in a coma for six hours. But seemingly unconscious, he'd actually awakened out of the body, in the inner worlds.

He lay in a coma for six hours. But seemingly unconscious, he'd actually awakened out of the body, in the inner worlds.

A realm of stunning beauty greeted him. There he found delightful rest and peace. His was a flood of bliss and ecstasy. And in that place of unspeakable love, Lenny caught sight of his neighbor, who'd been struck by lightning and translated (died). The man was lingering near a stairway leading to an even greater light. He motioned Lenny to join him; they'd ascend the stairs together. But Lenny shook his head. No, there was still plenty to see and do on earth.

Then a man with a snowy beard and in a long white robe addressed him. Was this God? (Lenny was to learn later that this exalted being would never, ever make a pretense of being God.) The old man spoke of the changes to come for Lenny: his future.

Lenny met other beings too. One especially striking man had a gleaming bald head, but more about that later.

Lenny could recall only fragments of his inner conversations with those beings, though the beauty and tranquility of that world were like an exquisite script engraved upon his heart. His remembrance of that celestial place enfolded him in an aura of peace and contentment. So profound and pure, in fact, was this recollection that he would spend many fruitless years trying either to recapture or escape its memory.

Lenny regained consciousness. He told his marvelous story to all who'd listen—friends, family, doctors, and nurses. Before long his doctors called in a psychologist, who cautioned him. "Don't speak of this," he said. "Put it behind you. Try to reenter society as a productive member."

To the psychologist, no doubt, it was probably just a hallucination brought on by stress or medical treatment. There was a place for people like that, and if Lenny didn't stop talking about the people and things he'd seen while unconscious, he'd land in a different kind of hospital.

Lenny took the hint. He quickly obeyed the Law of Silence and said no more about the matter.

Later Lenny's doctor would confide in him

A man with a snowy beard and in a long white robe addressed him. Was this God?

what a miracle his recovery had been. Such things did not happen; it was simply unheard of. The doctor, badly shaken by Lenny's amazing recovery, could not understand how he ever survived. It defied all reason.

For the next twenty years Lenny tried to blot his near-death experience from memory. He desperately wanted to get on with living, yet the exquisite splendor of that divine love continued to haunt him. So Lenny felt like a misfit in society.

A few months after leaving the hospital, he received a gift of an ECK book from a friend, but his interest was so-so. The ECK teachings would only cause friction in his family. Besides, the ECK beliefs appeared to be much different from those of his youth. Ah, better to let them go. And life rolled on.

Ten years later, tragedy struck again.

Lenny's best friend suffered a massive heart attack and died in his arms. The shock of it brought to mind memories of his own near-death experience. No question about it, his friend was rejoicing in the very love and peace that Lenny had once enjoyed too. Every waking hour since his best friend's death, Lenny tried to recapture that elusive feeling of total love and acceptance.

Even during this storm of pain and turmoil, Lenny could feel a guiding hand directing his affairs.

A few years ago, Lenny's own life began to unravel. For one, his marriage crumbled. Then, his career went up in smoke; he'd lost everything worth living for. Gone. Everything was gone. Yet even during this storm of pain and turmoil, Lenny could feel a guiding hand directing his affairs.

Who or what was this silent presence?

One day, seized by despair while out driving, Lenny cried, "What's going on? Help me! I give up! Do with me what you will. I need help!"

At that very moment, a white car swerved in front of him. Its bumper sticker read: "ECKANKAR 1-800-LOVE GOD." *Curious,* he thought.

Soon he began to notice those bumper stickers everywhere.

Tossing and turning one night, Lenny realized he was spiritually on the edge of a precipitous cliff. He would either plunge into a cold, dark hole, or he would soar into warm, life-giving sunshine. Which would it be? He crawled from under his covers and switched on the TV. On the screen, was an ad for the ECK Worldwide Seminar in Minneapolis, Minnesota. A voice inside him said, "Call the number." Lenny hesitated. "Call the number!" So he dialed 1-800-LOVE GOD.

A voice inside him said, "Call the number."

A short while later, a mailing arrived from Eckankar. Inside it was a free book, *ECKANKAR— Ancient Wisdom for Today.* He skimmed it; he liked it. All right, then, it was time to visit the Temple of ECK.

The Temple of ECK in Chanhassen, Minnesota, serves as both a worldwide Golden Wisdom Temple and a community church. This temple is Eckankar's spiritual home on earth. A special place, it stands as an outer symbol for the holy temple of God within every heart. Visitors often comment upon a very definite, loving presence there, for it reflects and rings with the subtle Light and Sound of God. Many visitors from around the world recognize they're in a unique, holy place. So they return again and again to renew their spiritual lives.

Lenny, a Minnesota resident, had driven past the temple for ten years. He'd always known he'd stop in someday, but a certain timidity kept him from it.

The temple was only fifteen minutes from home. But by the time he arrived, doubts had begun to prey on his determination. So he dallied in the parking lot to muster courage. *Why am I doing this?* he wondered. He finally overcame his reluctance and went into the building. Inside, a genial host offered him a tour, to which Lenny agreed. But the doubts persisted. He followed his host on the tour, still undecided whether to stay or go. The tour coursed along a corridor to a chapel near the main sanctuary. There, on a wall, hung color portraits of ECK Masters.

Lenny stared at them. For the first time since his near-death experience, he finally understood his out-of-the-body journey. He recognized the ECK Master Fubbi Quantz. He was the man with the white beard and long white robe. He was the very one Lenny had once mistaken for God, the one who'd told him things about his future.

And there, too, was a portrait of Yaubl Sacabi, the bald-headed man who'd offered guidance in times of trouble.

For the first time in twenty years, Lenny knew with absolute certainty that his experience had been real. He wasn't crazy; in fact, he was blessed.

For the first time since his near-death experience, he finally understood his out-of-the-body journey.

So Lenny brought home a copy of *The Shariyat-Ki-Sugmad*, the Eckankar bible, and read it cover to cover. That same night he completed an Eckankar membership form.

In so doing he agreed to let the Holy Spirit show him Its ways.

In good time, Lenny learned about karma, reincarnation, and past lives, and he also found answers to a lifetime of questions. Best of all, he discovered the way to again enter those worlds of light, love, and infinite beauty he'd seen so many long years ago. It is through the Spiritual Exercises of ECK.

Who, Why, and What You Are

A secret of spiritual doctrine is that God learns through you—rather, through your experiences as Soul.

God creates Souls and the many celestial spheres where they may have thousands upon thousands of adventures, and then waits to see what they learn while dashing from here to there. And, yes, God did add a freedom-giving but often troublemaking item to the resources of Soul: free will. It would either prove to be a flower or a thorn. Man could do as he liked, but he was fully responsible for his choices too.

You are a spark of God, of the same substance as the Holy Spirit, the Light and Sound.

So you are a spark of God, of the same substance as the Holy Spirit, the Light and Sound.

And your mission? It is to become a Co-worker with God.

Simple, so very simple, isn't it?

A Dream, Past Lives, and Healing

The dream teachings of ECK will open you to a clearer understanding of everyday problems, and at the same time give you real experiences to better realize the eternal, indestructible nature of Soul.

Why are dreams of such importance?

Why are dreams of such importance?

It always gets back to Soul, the Eternal Dreamer. We form our day-to-day existence through our creative imagination, Sugmad's gift to us. It is in our very nature to dream. That is why all your dreams, both in everyday life and while asleep, are of such importance. They are a crucial expression of the divine impulse to create that is showing itself in us.

Here, then, is Serena's story. She ably used her creative imagination to make a brighter, lighter future for herself.

Serena had suffered chronic neck pain since childhood. So she asked the Inner Master for a healing and by way of answer had both a dream and a past-life recall.

In the dream a man she could not stand had proposed marriage. Since he did this before an audience of her high-school classmates, she felt obliged to spare him from embarrassment. Reluctantly, then, she accepted. But the ring he slipped on her finger had no precious stone in its setting. Later in the dream, she recalled speaking with a girlfriend about the unwelcome proposal. Serena confided how much she despised him. Yet she felt paralyzed, trapped.

So the next morning Serena tested her creative

potential by doing a Spiritual Exercise of ECK. During it she met the Mahanta, who revealed how he was helping her unwind a long-standing karmic pattern.

Serena had been a nurse and healer in past lives. It was in this manner that she'd developed a tendency of taking on the pain of others. Even so, what had begun as a natural expression of sympathy eventually became a burden and a scourge. Her pattern in this lifetime was to take on the grief and pain of others at the expense of her own well-being. What a karmic snare!

The dream was certainly showing that she'd wedded herself to a self-destructive practice.

She later read this article in the *Mystic World*, a quarterly publication for ECK members: "Why People Don't Find Spiritual Freedom." In it, she recognized a duty to create her own happiness. She did want to change old patterns. How could she reach the source of her problem?

She recognized a duty to create her own happiness. She did want to change old patterns.

For that reason Serena handed this karmic situation to the Mahanta and has since noticed a great weight come off her shoulders. She has finally recognized that the origin of her trying to please and care for the illnesses of others was but a mask for her own desire to get a spiritual healing. Now her service to others is healthy and more satisfying too. She gives for love and no longer from a mistaken sense of obligation.

For all that, Serena learned there was more to come.

A different day in contemplation, the Inner Master brought to light Serena's past life as a religious figure in the early Christian era. She'd been a saintly woman, a nun. Her self-ordained mission was to convert prisoners, to try to save their souls before they were put to death. In this particular experience she saw herself in a long black habit. She marched resolutely on the heels of a prison guard who led the way to a murky dungeon and lit the dark passage with a smoky torch.

The pitiful wails of prisoners rose in the foul air. About to enter a cell armed only with her bible, Serena dismissed the guard with an arrogant wave of her hand.

"Stand back," she said. "I walk with God."

She then entered the cell alone, ready to do God's bidding with some poor wretch of a sinner. Unfortunately that day's poor wretch of a sinner had decided to sin again. As a result he brutally clubbed the unsuspecting nun in the back of her head and neck with the chains that bound his wrists. The injuries were fatal.

With the insights gained from her dream and contemplations, Serena could let go of her habit of taking on the emotional baggage of others.

Serena knew that this lifetime of pride in duty to save those she considered to be lesser Souls and the practice of taking on the emotional baggage of others were the reason for her chronic neck pain. She wanted to be rid of that burden from the past. So with the insights gained from her dream and contemplations, Serena could let go of her habit of taking on the emotional baggage of others. Moreover, she did physical exercises to strengthen her neck. Soon the pain was gone.

Serena thus learned a great secret: that her compulsion to save others was only an excuse to air her vanity. But she learned another fact. As her commitment to truth grows, the more she must give of God's love. Such was the great secret she'd learned from the Master.

Today Serena continues to walk with God, only now she does it much more wisely.

When we enter this world, we obtain certain abilities to carry us from cradle to grave. But if we choose to step on the spiritual path and make our way to God's kingdom, we have to earn a right to go there by learning other abilities.

So how do we do it?

We do it by learning to exercise our powers of imagination, to first visualize in great detail our world as we would have it. Everything around us today, from our choices in clothing to our placement with the family in which our rebirth occurred, is actually the outcome of attitudes we've formed over the centuries. We must form new attitudes if we wish to strike out in a new direction in our spiritual lives.

So how do we start?

We start to spiritualize our state of consciousness by learning the secrets of creative imagination. The doing of it comes through the Spiritual Exercises of ECK. In turn then, we see how upgrading our attitudes can bring into being a more pleasing and productive future for ourselves.

Everything around us today is actually the outcome of attitudes we've formed over the centuries.

How Julie Sidestepped a Family Feud

Each of us is unique in how we look at life, because our experiences are all our own. Even twins are unique; a different Soul exists in each human body, so their experiences in thought and feeling will necessarily be different too. As the Inner Master, I reach and teach many individuals at one and the same time. More important, I can speak to the understanding of each, to present the teachings of ECK in language that each can understand, no matter what his education or beliefs. I help people develop their creative self. They are then more able to follow out the ECK teachings to meet day-to-day troubles.

As the Inner Master, I reach and teach many individuals at one and the same time. I help people develop their creative self.

Julie, for example, was about to step right into the middle of a family feud. But before it could happen, she had a special dream.

In it, she was sitting in her den looking into the kitchen when she saw a tiny mouse creep from its hole in the wall. Gently she swept the mouse back into the hole with a broom. But the mouse grew in size; then it bit her. Julie screamed. She began to take vigorous swipes with the broom. Each attempt to corral the mouse made it grow ever larger until it had ballooned into a full-size rat. The dream turned into a nightmare; the rat began to overpower her. Julie cried for help, and the ECK came to the rescue: a ladder descended from somewhere above.

And just that quick, Julie scurried to the top of it and watched with relief, as the rat shrank in size, becoming an insignificant mouse again. It then fled into the hole from where it'd come.

This dream both intrigued and perplexed her.

The next morning in a spiritual exercise, Julie asked the Master what spiritual lesson there was to learn from it. The answer was: when a problem presented itself, she was to avoid confronting it head on. In the stress of the moment, she'd prove unable to use good judgment. Instead, she'd get drawn into the problem, and it would end up controlling her. Even worse, she'd fail to learn from the karma that had brought the situation upon her.

Being on top of the ladder represented to Julie that the ECK offered many levels of consciousness. There were choices in how to look at events. Julie realized the wisdom of avoiding the knee-jerk reactions of the human consciousness. It was far less taxing on the emotions to study instead the issues from the higher viewpoint of Soul, which would produce a much better outcome.

Now back to Julie's family feud.

Members of her family were fighting among themselves. This was not the first time Julie had let herself be dragged into an unhappy fray, since both sides of her family tried to enlist her in their arguments. She'd often played the part of peacemaker. Each side wanted her with them.

This time, however, Julie decided to remain on the sidelines.

She well remembered her dream lesson and instead stole to her room to sing HU. She formed no opinion about who was in the right or in the wrong.

Julie realized that in the past she'd become part of the problem, caught in the middle of family members by trying to be of help to them. But in this case she became a silent catalyst, as the two

Being on top of the ladder represented to Julie that the ECK offered many levels of consciousness. There were choices in how to look at events.

parties worked things out without her getting involved in a sticky, no-win karmic tangle. They had to resolve their own problems.

So her dream had been timely, highly instructive, and prophetic too. Her creative side had manifested in a very real manner via a spiritual dream.

Who Was the True Author of Doreen's Problems?

Doreen had a question for the Master: Was she herself the author of most of her problems?

Doreen, a Second Initiate, had a question for the Master: Was she herself the author of most of her problems?

One evening in bed she contemplated upon the question; that night she dreamed. The answer came in a dream that was to change her life forever.

She and a friend had set out to climb a mountain. The climb was very steep and rough, and her hands, feet, knees, and elbows were sore and bleeding from her many spills on the rugged and undeveloped path up the mountain. She strongly wished to quit, but her friend wouldn't hear of it. So she resolutely struggled on.

Finally, they topped the mountain. Oh, what a glorious sight! Both stood awestruck at a marvelous thing that now greeted their eyes.

A grand marble staircase ascended from the mountaintop and vanished into the clouds above. They began to climb the stairs. At the top they emerged into a fabulous garden that quite stole their breath. Flowers, hundreds of flowers, fra-

grant and of countless dazzling colors, drew but-
terflies, bees, dragonflies, hummingbirds, and
more. Songbirds soared and dipped in the sky. A
school of fish leaped playfully from the garden's
waterfall.

But the best was yet to come. In fact, what
followed would be the answer to her question that
evening at bedtime: Was she herself the author of
most of her problems?

Tiny lights danced about. They must have been
there the whole time, but the other amazing sights
had commanded their full attention. These lights
had no faces. Yet Doreen could recognize each as
a dear friend from the past. They spoke of their
love for each other through the language of Soul,
a superior kind of telepathy.

"Journey with us," the lights urged Doreen
and her friend. So not a moment later they were
in Soul form too.

They flew over vast oceans and lands. More
unbelievable scenes met their wondering sight,
like angels attending to both animals and people
in need. Even more compelling were the Souls
leaving their old bodies to enter fresh ones.

Returning to the garden, the two met Z, the
spiritual name of the Dream Master. He was in his
spiritual body, a brilliant ball of white light.

Z said to Doreen, "You have an important mission. Are you ready to help with that mission?"

"What is the mission?" she asked.

"Have faith and trust," he said. "You'll know
soon enough. The answer will come through love."

Then Z reached out with a hand of white light

*"What is
the mission?"
she asked.
He said,
"You'll know
soon enough.
The answer
will come
through love."*

and touched her heart, and with his love there also came the love of Sugmad. His touch had unleashed an unquenchable love and joy from deep inside her heart: She loosed a flood of tears.

Upon awakening, Doreen sobbed for hours on end. All the next week the mere thought of that remarkable dream of love brought more tears. Love—pure and unsullied love—was what she'd searched for her entire lifetime.

So what did Doreen learn from this dream?

Soul never dies. And, yes, she was indeed the author of most of her problems; but fortunately, she'd also found Eckankar, the ancient, yet ever-new, path to love and truth. Doreen felt at home there, at home among her friends at last.

Out of the Body after Final Exams

It's the privilege of every ECK Master to open a seeker's eyes to the eternal being he is, of the same substance as the Divine Spirit. I reach out to everyone who wishes to become a master of the laws of life, which will help him attain God Consciousness while still on earth. The individual enjoys a special relationship with Sugmad, his maker. He fully understands, then, how he is fashioned in the image of God. He also comes to know what this means by entering a new life of a once unimaginable love as he continues to walk among earth's sleeping and love-starved throngs.

So when someone begins to earnestly ask, What is love?—he's then ready to learn about the Light and Sound of God.

When someone begins to earnestly ask, What is love?—he's then ready to learn about the Light and Sound of God.

Years ago Julia, a college student, crammed two nights in a row to prepare for final exams. The third day she completed the last of them. Near exhaustion, she went straight home to rest, and seconds after her head hit the pillow, Julia was in slumberland. But then something quite extraordinary occurred: she was suddenly out of her body.

There she stood, off to one side of the bed, studying her room. She also inspected her human body, an inert cloak on the bed. An odd thought came to mind: *Should she phone her mother to let her know? Know what?*

Did I die? she wondered. That would certainly be news and worth a call.

This was Julia's first out-of-the-body experience. She didn't know that the Mahanta, the Living ECK Master was on hand, though invisible, to protect her from astral influences. Yet she did feel a definite mantle of love and protection around her.

Something away from the bed now caught her eye. Outside her bedroom window appeared a column of blazing blue-white light. It was six to eight feet around and filled her entire vision. There came a sound too. Much like a rushing wind, it nevertheless had more of a pulsing, electrical tone.

Then Julia awoke in bed again, fully united with her human body.

Many years would pass yet before she would actually meet the Master who introduced her to the Light and Sound of ECK on that day of final exams.

Julia's is one of many ways that the love of

Outside her bedroom window appeared a column of blazing blue-white light. There came a sound too, much like a rushing wind.

ECK comes to those who wish it. Religious experiences, like those reported in the Bible, are alive and well, continuing since the days of yore. Nor have they existed only as the singular experiences of saints; unsung average people, like Julia, continue to have them too.

A spiritual teaching that is alive and well still offers such experiences in the Light and Sound of God here and now. They are a necessary part of a true disciple's life. There are probably more people with this kind of experience in Eckankar than in any other religious group in the world.

The Miraculous Power of Your Imagination

Soul is a reflection of the ECK, for It was created from this Spirit and given the free will to make choices. Soul's attributes include both intelligence and imagination, and hence It can postulate and create things. It is the spark of eternal being that God has tucked within human and other material forms to animate them. As a result, Soul is like God in that It enjoys an inventive nature that sees no limitations.

Soul is like God in that It enjoys an inventive nature that sees no limitations.

The creative imagination is Sugmad's special gift to us, which develops along two lines: the mental and spiritual. The spiritual line creates things of a higher and finer nature than anything the mind could ever conceive of. The mind, on the other hand, is at its finest when it is like a surgical tool for the projects of Soul.

The creative imagination is vital in that it gives

people a way to help bring the greatest spiritual blessings into their lives. So what begins as imagination ends as a doorway to heaven. Yet it can influence the workings in this world too.

What begins as imagination ends as a doorway to heaven. Yet it can influence the workings in this world too.

Let's look now at Sally's problem and how she got help to make it right.

Sally had had trouble with her right foot and leg ever since she was a child; she'd suffered everything from sprains to serious injuries that sometimes even meant surgery. Sally is married now and works as a secretary. But she's still encumbered by that old nemesis, the weakened limb, which has become even a greater concern with each passing year. It made life as a wage earner much more of a challenge; worse, she'd just sprained that right ankle again. So to cheer her up, her husband brought home an orchid with nine flowers in full bloom. She loved its beauty. It helped check her self-pity at a critical juncture in her career.

Just an hour before dinner that same evening, Sally had written her monthly initiate report to the Mahanta, the Living ECK Master.

Just what is an initiate report? It is a written account that tells the Master of dreams and other experiences that've given its author a new insight into some personal quandary. The report allows free use of one's imagination, to review the past month from every angle and then sort the spiritual insights into some kind of order.

So in her report, Sally detailed her growing frustration that rose from the distress her sprained ankle was causing at work.

After dinner that evening she and her husband drew their chairs close to the resplendent orchid to do their nightly Spiritual Exercise of ECK. They first took a moment to admire the plant, and tears welled in Sally's eyes. The word *defective* kept coming to mind. She, in fact, felt defective. Did the Mahanta and Sugmad see her like that too?

The couple then began to sing HU, which, you certainly know by now, is an ancient name for God, a simple yet beautiful song of prayer to the Almighty.

Sally's awareness began to open to a past life.

Sally's awareness began to open to a past life. Born somewhere in the Middle East, she was then a boy with a clubfoot and a deformed right leg— the same side that had caused so much grief in this lifetime. Her past-life family had abandoned her in the desert to perish because of that defective limb. Soon, however, a caravan came to the rescue, only to enslave her in other cruel, heartrending surroundings. Sally recalled that past life with a shudder. It was an incarnation of pain and severe hardship, for her rescuers had treated her like a defective human being.

Strong feelings of being defective, then, had carried over into the present life. They accounted for her feelings of inferiority at work. She thought of herself as only a secretary, only capable of menial work, a thought that made her blood boil at her employer. A sense of being his slave nearly crushed her spirit.

Two days after she'd written her spiritual report to the Mahanta asking for help to understand that feeling of inferiority, her ankle began to heal at last. She further recognized the spiritual value of her secretarial duties. They were giving her strength, preparing her for the next leg of her journey home to God.

Her monthly report detailing her problem is one example of the creative imagination in expression.

The Master's response to her letter, which she'd written but not yet mailed, was like the cry of a hawk: a sharp whistle that cut through her self-pity. It awakened her to a higher state of awareness. He'd let her see a key past life that gave meaning to what had seemed like undue pain and drudgery in the present.

The Master let her see a key past life that gave meaning to what had seemed like undue pain and drudgery in the present.

Moreover, the gift of the orchid had opened her heart. It is ever true that healings occur easiest in an atmosphere of love.

Imagination is the God-spark within you. It is the only gift of God that we can rightly lay claim to in the physical body, this gift of imagination. So learn to use its full powers. Put creative imagination into all your spiritual exercises. It, with the Master's help, can set aside blocks to our well-being put there by a meddlesome mind.

The creative imagination is one thing that can lift us into truly becoming godlike beings.

Was It Really Soul Travel?

Gloria once had a one-on-one case study with the Mahanta on the creative imagination. She had been experimenting with it in her spiritual exercise. It is a practice she does for twenty minutes every day before going to work.

One morning Gloria was led to the Oracle of Tirmer. It is in the Valley of Shangta, a sacred gathering place for ECK Masters and others who may come only by express invitation of the Mahanta. The Master showed her a place to sit in a theaterlike setting amid the rocky landscape. Then ECK Master Gopal Das approached, and she jumped to her feet.

"Hello, dear friend!" he said.

Her heart sang with pleasure. He did remember her!

They'd met, oh, so many long years ago, so long ago that it seemed like ages and ages. Years before Gloria had found the outer path of ECK, she used to see and talk with Gopal Das in her dreams.

After this experience with Gopal Das in the Valley of Shangta, Gloria began to second-guess the reality of this meeting with him.

After this experience with Gopal Das in the Valley of Shangta, Gloria began to second-guess the reality of this meeting with him. It was probably nothing more substantial than a figment of a fertile imagination.

Boy, what an imagination! Even thinking that such a great ECK Master would greet me . . .

The mind had raised considerable doubts, determined to reduce a real spiritual experience to the frivolous play of a fanciful imagination. But the Inner Master knows how to get around such common obstacles to spiritual freedom. He laid out a plan.

How did it manifest for Gloria?

The very next day, as usual, Gloria sang the HU song to begin her spiritual exercises. To her surprise, try as she might to mock up an image of Gopal Das on the inner screen of her mind, she saw nothing at all. Not a thing.

And so the Mahanta had dissolved her impression of the day before (that she'd only imagined meeting Gopal Das) because today she could imagine nothing at all.

Gloria thanked him. He was letting her see that the wonderful experiences that came from using one's creative imagination for Soul Travel were indeed real and worth the time and effort. So, too, were the companionship of the ECK Masters and her explorations of the God Worlds.

He was letting her see that the wonderful experiences that came from using one's creative imagination for Soul Travel were indeed real.

What Lay behind Marcus's Addiction to Sugar

The Holy Spirit will lift you spiritually via the Sugmad's agent, the Mahanta, the Living ECK Master, who opens the Third Eye to let in the Light and Sound of God. It brings about your purification, which allows karma to resolve and wash away.

Next, we see what power the Master's mercy has on a chela's determination to conquer a habit of long duration, which had strengthened and created a spiritual impasse for its hapless victim.

Marcus had had an addiction to sugar all his forty-some years. Long in its tenacious hold, he had tried many times to be rid of it. This addiction lessened his well-being in countless ways, leaving him to feel helpless and, well, consumed. Once, after binging on a whole box of cookies, he began to weep in resignation. How could he beat his sugar addiction? It was killing him, but he just couldn't stop eating sweets. All his efforts had failed. So he asked the Mahanta for help.

One morning in contemplation, he had an exhilarating experience in which the Master lifted him to the Soul Plane itself. There Wah Z showed him three cards; they depicted three past lives of Marcus. In two of them Marcus was entangled by the meshes of alcoholism.

"These past lives are contributing to your addiction," the Master said. "Here's the one that started it all."

Wah Z showed him a past life in the Far East when he'd introduced unfortunate Souls to the use of drugs. That is a serious spiritual crime. And it makes no difference if society's laws permit their use.

"I am going to help you with this," Wah Z said.

Then he removed the card for that past life and guided Marcus through his Mental, Causal, Astral, and Physical bodies. The Master deftly removed all the residual energies and engrams produced by that misspent lifetime.

To his great relief, Marcus found that his sugar cravings were now something he could control; he could get on with his life. And he has done so, grateful for the help of the Master to do what he himself could not.

"I now know what the mercy in the Ocean of Love and Mercy means," he says.

The Ocean of Love and Mercy is a term to describe the home of God. Aflame with the

> *"These past lives are contributing to your addiction," the Master said. "Here's the one that started it all."*

Master's love for his healing, Marcus was inspired to continue his journey home to God.

More on the ECK Initiations

Many kinds of fears hide in people's inner pockets, but people zip the pockets shut and pretend they just aren't there. But they are there, always ready to brew trouble.

A more common name for these fears is karma. Rather, we tremble at the unsettling aftermath of karma—the pain, fear, and loneliness. On the path of ECK, the Mahanta, the Living ECK Master, via spiritual exercises, begins to uncover these fears one by one. Hence an individual can get used to the changes made for his betterment. And with each new initiation in ECK, more of his leftover karma passes into the Audible Life Stream (the Holy Spirit, the ECK). And as this karmic weight lifts, a new sense of freedom and happiness sweeps into the individual's life.

As a result, each initiation is a dynamic part of winning full spiritual freedom.

As each initiate passes into a new circle of initiation, he finds many, many different avenues for unfoldment within that circle. Each avenue leads to a test, much like in a regular classroom.

Each initiation is a dynamic part of winning full spiritual freedom.

Can someone fake the answers to these tests? Would he fool the Master with, "Well, I'm all over my lust. No more tests here, right?"

Wrong. The Master decides when a disciple is ready for a new initiation. Impatience gets the disciple nowhere.

But if the individual lets a mutual trust develop between himself and the ECK, he soon finds that It is always working for him. The Master, the ECK, designs each test as an opportunity for spiritual growth. So every single moment of one's life benefits from the Master's ever-present love and protection. No spiritual harm can ever befall him. The shield of God is always at his side, ready to protect him from all spiritual harm.

The ECK initiation joins Soul with the eternal, life-giving Sound Current. Old karma comes to an end, and the individual finds life to be a rich, restyled experience, much different from pre-ECK days. The sure hand of the Mahanta guides him by the moment.

The ECK initiation joins Soul with the eternal, life-giving Sound Current.

Rose's First Initiation

Now let's look at Rose's First Initiation, which the Mahanta gave her in a dream. It is a landmark in one's spiritual life.

Rose had known that her First Initiation in ECK was soon to be, so she paid close attention to her dreams. Rose carefully noted the character of her dreams. Many had to do with water—oceans, bathing, lapping and consuming waves, rivers, and even swimming pools.

Water, it should be noted, is often a sign of purification.

In one memorable instance, a dream showed Rose and her daughter sitting on a sofa before a large picture window. Her daughter had just remarked on how beautiful Rose looked, with honey blond hair glistening in the light. Then the outside door blew wide open. A torrent of silver rain swept in, quickly turning into a golden shower that swirled about the room. At this, Rose opened her eyes. She could still see the golden shower in her bedroom, but now it was forming into the shapes of golden hearts. What a remarkable sight! Instinctively she shut her eyes again, but the light had stolen away, leaving only the sweet, delicate kiss of God's love.

Another morning, for just a brief moment, while she still lay in bed with eyes shut, Rose clearly saw the word *beloved* written in the Blue Light of the Mahanta. Both experiences assured her that love for ECK indeed returns to one a hundredfold.

So the Mahanta, in a most delightful and enriching way, had honored her request to remember her first ECK initiation.

At this, Rose opened her eyes. She could still see the golden shower but now it was forming into the shapes of golden hearts.

The Boatman

An ECK Master may approach someone who's still in childhood, but then the shutter of memory closes on the event until that person learns of ECK again later in life. Nancy's story illustrates this point.

Nancy tells of her first encounter with the Mahanta when she was around eight and in the third grade. She remembered falling asleep at bedtime and then hearing a voice she believed to be God calling her name. Other than that, she could never remember any of her dreams.

However, one night there came a dream she would remember the rest of her life.

She found herself walking to school with friends when the road suddenly turned into an ocean. A sailboat appeared as the waves began to briskly dance. The man in the boat was wearing a yellow slicker, complete with hood and protective brim. Nancy peered into the smiling eyes of this mysterious fellow as he reached for her hand in welcome.

"Come aboard," he said.

She grasped his hand. She knew that a sailing adventure would meet heavy seas at times, but she'd get through that with the help of this kind friend. He turned to her friends on shore.

"Would any of you like to come aboard?" All shook their heads.

To her amazement, Nancy discovered a picture of the very man from her long-ago dream. He'd been her guide since childhood, and now she finally knew his name.

In the morning, Nancy did remember this dream. She had a feeling that at some later date, when she was grown, its full significance would come to her, and she would understand the meaning of this dream.

Nineteen years later, Nancy was at a new company where a supervisor treated her with great kindness; he was an exceptional listener. Their conversations often ran to uplifting topics. One day he invited her to a spiritual discussion class. To her amazement, Nancy there discovered a picture of the very man from her long-ago dream—the Mahanta, the Living ECK Master, Wah Z. He'd been her guide throughout all the ups and downs of her life since childhood, and now she finally knew his name. He could help show her who she was, to fulfill her destiny as a spark of God.

So Nancy became a member of ECK.

A Dream of Prophecy

Dreams of prophecy are alive and well today, even as they were in the Old Testament. This is especially true among ECKists. Such dreams can also help one resolve old karma.

Some of these dreams of prophecy had come to Faith, showing her she'd qualify for two educational programs. So she applied for them. Faith had no doubt she'd be accepted for both. And true to her dreams, the school had accepted her for both programs.

So Faith trusts the power of her dreams.

Another dream warned that her boyfriend would start an argument and ask her to leave the apartment they shared. And, indeed, it played out just as her dream had said. He asked her to leave and stormed from the house. So she started packing.

Faith had wanted to leave him for two years, but the Mahanta had told her it wasn't yet time.

She was to be out of the house by the time her boyfriend returned. But midway through packing, the Mahanta's voice said very clearly that she could stop packing, because her boyfriend would apologize when he returned and would ask her to stay. She's come to have much confidence in the Master, so she did as he suggested and quit packing. But her mind whispered, "But what if he doesn't ask you to stay?"

So Faith was ready for anything, prepared to leave if her boyfriend had had no change of heart. Of course, events turned out just as the Mahanta had foreseen.

Dreams of prophecy are alive and well today, even as they were in the Old Testament.

Faith realized that a continued relationship was the most pleasant way to work out old karma with her boyfriend.

Bill's Dream Helps an Old Friend

Bill was the assistant headmaster at a school. He'd attended an introductory program on Eckankar where he'd received a picture of the Mahanta, the Living ECK Master along with some ECK reading material.

One day a friend of Bill's came to the school and asked that his son be added to the admissions list. But Bill couldn't help him: the list was full. The friend left disappointed.

At day's end, however, Bill had an idea. He'd test the validity of the Inner Master. He looked at the Master's picture and said, "If you are indeed the Wayshower and Inner Master, you should help me so I can help my friend."

That night Bill had a dream. The Inner Master appeared and said he should recheck the admissions list.

That night Bill had a dream. The Inner Master appeared and said he should recheck the admissions list. He drew Bill's attention to a name written twice on the list.

Bill did as his dream had advised. And there *was* that name entered twice on the admissions list, just as the Inner Master had said. He corrected the error and called his friend to report the good news: his son could enroll in the school after all.

After his experience Bill told people in his community how practical Eckankar is, and now everyone there wants to have the Master's picture and also learn more about Eckankar.

Bill is thinking about becoming an ECKist too.

Why Our Biggest Disappointments May Happen

Even the most disappointing experience in our life may have a higher purpose set in motion by the Holy Spirit. So says Jane, an ECKist whose story follows.

Even the most disappointing experience in our life may have a higher purpose set in motion by the Holy Spirit.

Jane got a phone call from Jim, an old college boyfriend, who'd spent considerable time in tracking her down. She'd known him only a year. Financial reasons had forced her to quit college at the end of the year, so they had said good-bye. It was a sad parting, but it had been a major loss for Jim. He felt all his life that he'd missed something important.

Jim had married a college classmate and they'd raised two sons. When the boys went off to college, Jim had also paid the full tuition for both their girlfriends, for he'd become a very successful businessman.

"So they wouldn't lose the girls they loved the way I lost you," he told Jane.

At the end of their two-and-a-half-hour phone conversation, Jim said, "Don't ever forget that there are two young woman teaching school today because of you."

That night she contemplated on the phone call to learn its significance. In the morning she had a bigger picture. As mentioned above, she learned that even the most disappointing things in life may be a part of the Holy Spirit's plan to bring about some good. If she'd married Jim, her life would have turned out completely different. She might never have found ECK. But now, the phone call had cut the last thread of karma between them.

Jane says, "There's more to being a vehicle for the ECK than any of us can fully understand and put into words."

Which Way Now?

Your experiences here on earth offer a chance to develop the beauty and grace necessary for a Co-worker with God. When the season is right, each of us finds the ancient, yet ever-new, teachings of ECK and can now set out on the most ecstatic adventure of a lifetime, the journey to God.

When the season is right, each of us finds the ancient, yet ever-new, teachings of ECK and can now set out on the most ecstatic adventure of a lifetime.

All of us must make dozens and dozens of which-way-now? decisions at important crossroads during the course of our many lifetimes. But at the end of the road is the Mahanta, who receives all with great joy. And we're never again alone from that moment on.

The route to light and truth is quicker for some than others. All depends upon Soul's determination.

What is life other than us meeting ourselves in the play of the world? The odyssey of Soul teaches us to cooperate with the laws of God. When we've learned to do that, the highest, purest, and finest love in all the far-flung worlds of God is ours. You may be sure that this spiritual odyssey is worth every single moment.

A Spiritual Exercise on the Mountain of God

This is a technique of the imagination.

Find a quiet place for this spiritual exercise where no one will disturb you for ten or fifteen minutes. Then shut your eyes and look behind and between your eyebrows. That is the location of your Spiritual Eye.

Now imagine you are climbing to the top of a broad green mountain. Follow the dirt path that leads to a meadow dressed in a carpet of bright, cheerful flowers. Powder white clouds kiss the summit of the mountain and will instill in you a sense of great joy and wonder.

That is the Mountain of God.

When you reach the top, lie upon the thick, soft carpet of luxurious grass. Feel the sunshine play on your face, arms, and body. Now shut your eyes there on the mountain, too, as you did at the beginning of this spiritual exercise.

Then look gently but steadily into your Spiritual Eye for the Light of God. While waiting for It to appear, sing HU slowly, again and again.

The Light may appear as a soft field of light, similar to the soft white clouds above the mountain. Or it may be a pinpoint of light—blue, white, yellow, purple, or even green or pink.

Look gently but steadily into your Spiritual Eye for the Light of God. While waiting for It to appear, sing HU slowly, again and again.

Continue to watch for the Light within your Spiritual Eye. Now also start listening for the Sound of God.

The Sound of God is simply the vibration of the Holy Spirit moving the atoms of life. So you may hear It as the sound of a flute, a rushing wind, the chirping of birds, a crashing waterfall, ringing bells, or the buzzing of bees. These are actual, not imaginary, sounds.

After ten or fifteen minutes, stop the spiritual exercise if you've not heard or seen something. Repeat this exercise tomorrow and every day thereafter for a month, or until you get results.

The sole purpose of this exercise is to awaken you to the Light and Sound of God.

The sole purpose of this exercise is to awaken you to the Light and Sound of God. This dual manifestation of the Voice of God can bring you more love, wisdom, and understanding. Return to the Mountain of God a few minutes every day. This imaginative journey in contemplation is one of the surest ways to arrive there soon in full consciousness.

A Final Word

*N*ow you know something about a few of those wonderful ECK Masters. You've met the golden-haired Gopal Das, who once served the spiritual needs of the ancient Egyptians.

And you've met Fubbi Quantz, too, the guardian of the Katsupari Monastery. And Rebazar Tarzs, who comes to life on the pages of Paul Twitchell's book *Stranger by the River.* Lai Tsi, you recall, is the wise and tranquil Chinese ECK Master who finds a special pleasure in helping seekers along the spiritual path.

There's Kata Daki. She and an untold number of other women ECK Masters also aspire to lift the vision of seekers to the higher states of consciousness.

Not to forget Shamus-i-Tabriz. He was a friend and mentor of the genius poet Jalal ad-Din ar-Rumi in early Persia. And let's not overlook any of the other great ECK Masters. Every one of them loves people, even as God loves all beings. Numbered among the ECK Masters, too, are the African Towart Managi. And Rami Nuri, who is literally out of this world, on Venus. Paul Twitchell, the erstwhile Cliff Hanger and founder of today's

Every one of the great ECK Masters loves people, even as God loves all beings.

275

Eckankar, is also among those renowned ECK Masters. Wah Z, yours truly, serves as the current Mahanta, the Living ECK Master.

So you've met all those ECK Masters here and have read stories of how they've helped others like you. When you're ready for something more durable than philosophy, metaphysics, or orthodox religion, then you're ready for the knowledge that grants love, wisdom, and spiritual freedom. These three qualities are available through the teachings of ECK. And if you appreciate what you've learned in these pages, you are welcome to join this most grand journey to your Creator.

May the blessings be.

When you're ready, love, wisdom, and spiritual freedom are available through the teachings of ECK.

Glossary

Words set in SMALL CAPS are defined elsewhere in this glossary.

BLUE LIGHT. How the MAHANTA often appears in the inner worlds to the CHELA or seeker.

CHELA. *CHEE-lah* A spiritual student. Often refers to a member of ECKANKAR.

ECK. *EHK* The Life Force, the Holy Spirit, or Audible Life Current which sustains all life.

ECKANKAR. *EHK-ahn-kahr* Religion of the Light and Sound of God. Also known as the Ancient Science of SOUL TRAVEL. A truly spiritual religion for the individual in modern times. The teachings provide a framework for anyone to explore their own spiritual experiences. Established by PAUL TWITCHELL, the modern-day founder, in 1965. The word means "Co-worker with God."

ECK MASTER(S). Spiritual Masters who can assist and protect people in their spiritual studies and travels. The ECK Masters are from a long line of God-Realized SOULS who know the responsibility that goes with spiritual freedom.

ECK RITE OF PASSAGE. One of the Four ECK Celebrations of Life. This ceremony is for youth on the threshold of becoming adults, at about age thirteen. It celebrates a personal commitment to the ECK teachings, to accepting the presence of the MAHANTA, and to becoming more aware of one's true spiritual nature.

GOD-REALIZATION. The state of God Consciousness. Complete and conscious awareness of God.

HU. *HYOO* The most ancient, secret name for God. The singing of the word *HU* is considered a love song to God. It can be sung aloud or silently to oneself.

INITIATION. Earned by a member of ECKANKAR through spiritual unfoldment and service to God. The initiation is a private ceremony in which the individual is linked to the Sound and Light of God.

277

KARMA. LAW OF. The Law of Cause and Effect, action and reaction, justice, retribution, and reward, which applies to the lower or psychic worlds: the Physical, Astral, Causal, Mental, and Etheric Planes.

KAL NIRANJAN, THE. *KAL nee-RAHN-jahn* The Kal; the negative power, also known as Satan or the devil.

KLEMP, HAROLD. The present MAHANTA, the LIVING ECK MASTER. SRI Harold Klemp became the Mahanta, the Living ECK Master in 1981. His spiritual name is WAH Z.

LIVING ECK MASTER. The title of the spiritual leader of ECKANKAR. His duty is to lead SOUL back to God. The Living ECK Master can assist spiritual students physically as the Outer Master, in the dream state as the Dream Master, and in the spiritual worlds as the Inner Master.

MAHANTA. *mah-HAHN-tah* A title to describe the highest state of God Consciousness on earth, often embodied in the LIVING ECK MASTER. He is the Living Word. An expression of the Spirit of God that is always with you.

MAHDIS. *MAH-dees* The initiate of the Fifth Circle (SOUL PLANE); often used as a generic term for all High Initiates in ECK.

PLANE(S). The levels of existence, such as the Physical, Astral, Causal, Mental, Etheric, and SOUL Planes.

SATSANG. *SAHT-sahng* A class in which students of ECK study a monthly lesson from ECKANKAR.

SELF-REALIZATION. SOUL recognition. The entering of Soul into the Soul PLANE and there beholding Itself as pure Spirit. A state of seeing, knowing, and being.

SHARIYAT-KI-SUGMAD. *SHAH-ree-aht-kee-SOOG-mahd* The sacred scriptures of ECKANKAR. The scriptures are comprised of about twelve volumes in the spiritual worlds. The first two were transcribed from the inner PLANES by PAUL TWITCHELL, modern-day founder of ECKANKAR.

SOUL. The True Self. The inner, most sacred part of each person. Soul exists before birth and lives on after the death of the physical body. As a spark of God, Soul can see, know, and perceive all things. It is the creative center of Its own world.

SOUL TRAVEL. The expansion of consciousness. The ability of SOUL to transcend the physical body and travel into the spiritual worlds of God. Soul Travel is taught only by the LIVING ECK MASTER. It helps people unfold spiritually and can provide proof of the existence of God and life after death.

Sᴏᴜɴᴅ ᴀɴᴅ Lɪɢʜᴛ ᴏғ ECK.   The Holy Spirit. The two aspects through which God appears in the lower worlds. People can experience them by looking and listening within themselves and through Sᴏᴜʟ Tʀᴀᴠᴇʟ.

Sᴘɪʀɪᴛᴜᴀʟ Exᴇʀᴄɪsᴇs ᴏғ ECK.   The daily practice of certain techniques to get us in touch with the Light and Sound of God.

Sʀɪ. *SREE*   A title of spiritual respect, similar to reverend or pastor, used for those who have attained the Kingdom of God. In Eᴄᴋᴀɴᴋᴀʀ, it is reserved for the Mᴀʜᴀɴᴛᴀ, the Lɪᴠɪɴɢ ECK Mᴀsᴛᴇʀ.

Sᴜɢᴍᴀᴅ. *SOOG-mahd*   A sacred name for God. Sugmad is neither masculine nor feminine; It is the source of all life.

Tᴇᴍᴘʟᴇs(s) ᴏғ Gᴏʟᴅᴇɴ Wɪsᴅᴏᴍ.   These Golden Wisdom Temples are spiritual temples which exist on the various ᴘʟᴀɴᴇs—from the Physical to the Anami Lok; ᴄʜᴇʟᴀs of Eᴄᴋᴀɴᴋᴀʀ are taken to the temples in the Sᴏᴜʟ body to be educated in the divine knowledge; the different sections of the Sʜᴀʀɪʏᴀᴛ-Kɪ-Sᴜɢᴍᴀᴅ, the sacred teachings of ECK, are kept at these temples.

Vᴀɪʀᴀɢ. *vie-RAHG* Detachment.

Wᴀʜ Z. *WAH zee*   The spiritual name of Sʀɪ Hᴀʀᴏʟᴅ Kʟᴇᴍᴘ. It means the Secret Doctrine. It is his name in the spiritual worlds.

For more explanations of Eᴄᴋᴀɴᴋᴀʀ terms, see *A Cosmic Sea of Words: The ECKANKAR Lexicon* by Harold Klemp.

For Further Reading and Study

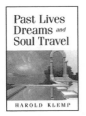

Past Lives, Dreams, and Soul Travel
Harold Klemp

What if you could recall past-life lessons for your benefit today? What if you could learn the secret knowledge of dreams to gain the wisdom of the heart? Or Soul Travel, to master the shift in consciousness needed to find peace and contentment? To ride the waves of God's love and mercy? Let Harold Klemp, leading authority in all three fields, show you how.

How to Survive Spiritually in Our Times, Mahanta Transcripts, Book 16
Harold Klemp

A master storyteller, Harold Klemp weaves stories, tips, and techniques into the golden fabric of his talks. They highlight the deeper truths within you, so you can apply them in your life *now*. He speaks right to Soul. It is that divine, eternal spark that you are. The survivor. Yet survival is only the starting point in your spiritual life. Harold Klemp also shows you how to gain in spiritual wealth. This book's a treasure.

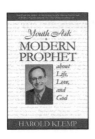

Youth Ask a Modern Prophet about Life, Love, and God
Harold Klemp

What am I here for? How do I find lasting love? When will my karma be finished? Do these questions sound familiar? The youth of today aren't afraid to voice these important questions, and many more, to Harold Klemp. His answers are candid and wise with practical solutions. You will find great value in this book no matter your age.

The Spiritual Exercises of ECK
Harold Klemp
This book is a staircase with 131 steps. But you don't have to climb all the steps to get to the top. Each step is a spiritual exercise, a way to help you explore your inner worlds. And what awaits you at the top? The doorway to spiritual freedom, self-mastery, wisdom, and love.

The Spiritual Laws of Life
Harold Klemp
There exist truths—spiritual laws that guide and benefit us. How can we shape our lives and destiny to live in harmony with them? Discover how you can meet today's challenges in a more relaxed, awakened, and happy way. The spiritual laws of life give us many resources to make the best choices.

The Tiger's Fang
Paul Twitchell
Paul Twitchell's teacher, Rebazar Tarzs, takes him on a journey through vast worlds of Light and Sound, to sit at the feet of the spiritual Masters. Their dialogue brings out the secret of how to draw closer to God—and awaken Soul to Its spiritual destiny.

ECK Masters and You: An Illustrated Guide
Harold Klemp
How can these Co-workers with God help *you*? Discover the guidance, healing, protection, and divine love available through the ECK Masters since the beginning of time. Beautiful, full-color artwork illustrates this introduction to seven ECK Masters and the Golden Wisdom Temples where you can visit them. *Available spring 2006.*

Available at bookstores, online booksellers, or directly from Eckankar: www.eckankar.org; (952) 380-2222; ECKANKAR, Dept. BK57, PO Box 2000, Chanhassen, MN 55317-2000 USA.

There May Be an
Eckankar Study Group near You

Eckankar offers a variety of local and international activities for the spiritual seeker. With hundreds of study groups worldwide, Eckankar is near you! Many areas have Eckankar centers where you can browse through the books in a quiet, unpressured environment, talk with others who share an interest in this ancient teaching, and attend beginning discussion classes on how to gain the attributes of Soul: wisdom, power, love, and freedom.

Around the world, Eckankar study groups offer special one-day or weekend seminars on the basic teachings of Eckankar. For membership information, visit the Eckankar Web site (www.eckankar.org). For the location of the Eckankar center or study group nearest you, click on "Other Eckankar Web sites" for a listing of those areas with Web sites. You're also welcome to check your phone book under **ECKANKAR**; call **(952) 380-2222, Ext. BK57;** or write **ECKANKAR, Att: Information, BK57, PO Box 2000, Chanhassen, MN 55317-2000 USA.**

☐ Please send me information on the nearest Eckankar center or study group in my area.

☐ Please send me more information about membership in Eckankar, which includes a twelve-month spiritual study.

Please type or print clearly

Name _____
        first (given)   last (family)

Street _____ Apt. # _____

City_____ State/Prov. _____

Zip/Postal Code _____ Country _____

285

About the Author

Harold Klemp was born in Wisconsin and grew up on a small farm. He attended a two-room country schoolhouse before going to high school at a religious boarding school in Milwaukee, Wisconsin.

After preministerial college in Milwaukee and Fort Wayne, Indiana, he enlisted in the U.S. Air Force. There he trained as a language specialist at Indiana University and a radio intercept operator at Goodfellow AFB, Texas. Then followed a two-year stint in Japan where he first encountered Eckankar.

In October 1981, he became the spiritual leader of Eckankar, Religion of the Light and Sound of God. His full title is Sri Harold Klemp, the Mahanta, the Living ECK Master. As the Living ECK Master, Harold Klemp is responsible for the continued evolution of the Eckankar teachings.

His mission is to help people find their way back to God in this life. Harold Klemp travels to ECK seminars in North America, Europe, and the South Pacific. He has also visited Africa and many countries throughout the world, meeting with spiritual seekers and giving inspirational talks. There are many videocassettes and audiocassettes of his public talks available.

In his talks and writings, Harold Klemp's sense of humor and practical approach to spirituality have helped many people around the world find truth in their lives and greater inner freedom, wisdom, and love.

International Who's Who of Intellectuals
Ninth Edition